A LOOKOUT PUBLICATION

# SPAIN'S WILDLIFE

Eric Robins

Photography by José Luis Rodríguez

# ABOUT THE AUTHOR

*British author and journalist Eric Robins, who describes himself as "an enthusiastic amateur naturalist," has been studying the fauna of Iberia for more than a decade. Prior to that, he spent 25 years in Africa as a correspondent for Time-Life.*

*Robin's previous nine non-fiction books include among others Secret Eden (Hamish Hamilton/Elm Tree), Operation Noah (Taplinger/Herbert Jenkins); The Ebony Ark (Barrie & Jenkins); The Congo River (Coward-McCann); Africa: Images & Realities (Ridge Press, New York), and The Book of Kenya (Collins/Harvill).*

*Robins is a contributor to Reader's Digest, Lookout and a number of leading international magazines concerned with wildlife conservation and nature issues. He lives in southern Portugal with his wife, photographer Marion Kaplan.*

*To Marion*
*who is everything*

Photography by José Luis Rodríguez

Additional photography by José Luis González Grande (pages 131, 135); Helmich/J. L. Rodríguez (82); Marion Kaplan (29, 140-141, 144); Jean Louis Klein/J. L. Rodríguez (60-61, 76, 96); Carlos Sanz/J. L. Rodríguez (46, 49).

## ACKNOWLEDGEMENTS

The author is most grateful to the following for their guidance, cooperation or professional encouragement in the preparation and writing of this work:
Sahm Sefton; Allen and Margaret Rees; John Reader; Nigel Bowden; Marion Kaplan; Roberto Hartasanchez; Caroline Robins; Jill Jolliffe; the Secretary General of ADENA *(Asociación para la defensa de la naturaleza);* Ana Pinto de Sousa; Robert Lyle; the staff of the British Council library.

Many thanks also go to José Luis Rodríguez and his colleagues whose outstanding photographs have brought "Spain's Wildife" so vividly to life.

Printed by Pentacrom S.L. Miguel Yuste, 33. - 28037 Madrid
I.S.B.N.: 84-87112-04-8 D.L.: M-35350-1989

# CONTENTS

*"...Nature conservation is one of
the great public endeavours of our age..."*


—His Majesty King Juan Carlos I of Spain
March 27, 1989

FRANCE

CANTABRIAN MOUNTAINS

PYRENEES

GALICIA

ORDESA

PORTUGAL

CASTILLA-LEON

DELTA
DEL EBRO

SIERRA DE GREDOS

BALEARIC Is.

MADRID

MONFRAGÜE

ALBUFERA

EXTREMADURA

SIERRA MORENA

CAZORLA

ANDALUCIA

COTO
DOÑANA

FUENTE DE PIEDRA

MEDITERRANEAN SEA

*Previous pages: remote and wild, the natural park of Monfragüe in Extremadura harbours many of Spain's endangered species.*

# Introduction

**B**LACK bulls and glamorous matadors. Such is the instant image of Spain in the eyes of most foreigners.

Few people think of Spain as a wildlife wonderland, the last refuge in Europe for a host of exotic animals and birds. Spain is in fact a rich domain of fauna — the beautiful and the bizarre — thanks to the country's near-tropical location and geographical diversity, which provides a broad spectrum of natural habitats.

With some 190,000 square miles mainland Spain is Western Europe's largest country after France. It has more scenic and climatic variety (amounting, they say, to 15 different "Spains") than most other lands.

*Her natural wonders are far from the teeming coastal areas and tourist centres visited each year by tens of millions of holiday-makers from Britain, the United States, West Germany, France, Scandinavia and elsewhere. These vacation visitors, as a whole, see little of Spain's great patchwork of hidden beauties: snow-mantled mountains, almost as numerous as Switzerland's, and searing semi-deserts; cork-oak groves and broad wetlands; deep escarpments and grassy plains; tranquil lakes and lagoons; pine forests and granite precipices; wide rivers and valleys filled with shadows; turbulent trout streams and deep, dark salmon pools; caves with prehistoric paintings...*

*Living free within the borders of their vast, rugged Spanish home is a fascinating variety of wild creatures. Many of them are rare and threatened, and involved in a constant life-or-death struggle. They are pitched against creeping urbanisation, tourist developments, trophy hunters, ruthless egg collectors, deforestation for the paper trades, farmers with itchy trigger-fingers, industrial and agricultural poisons, cruel traps and snares, disastrous forest fires (many started deliberately), acid rain, the draining of marshes and wetlands for profit, illicit trading in animal skins and other threats such as those posed by nuclear wastes or mishaps, disastrous weather conditions caused by human agencies...*

*Even so Spain can still boast great ecological wealth among her peaks and plains, which provide relatively safe wildlife retreats and breeding sites. Unlike many other parts of our planet, the story of nature in Spain is by no means one of doom and gloom.*

*In the past, unbridled economic development seemed the principal consideration in government policy. But today the environment on which people once turned their backs is regarded as one of the country's greatest treasures.*

*Although, as someone has put it, "Spain woke up late to the environmental issue," it has in recent years made marked strides in maintaining wild places and their inhabitants.*

*The government now boasts on the mainland several large national parks (there are others on her islands) where the fauna is safeguarded by wardens and protection laws whose infringement is met with severe penalties.*

*The showpiece of these parks is the vast, internationally famous Coto Doñana park in the south, visited alike by premiers and parties of schoolchildren eager to view its hundreds of species of birds and other wild animals.*

*"Here," as writer Jan Morris describes Doñana so neatly, "the resources of pristine Spain are left unsnared, unshot and uneaten."*

*In 1981 the United Nations Educational, Scientific and Cultural Organization (Unesco) recognized Doñana as a "Reserve of the Biosphere."*

*In addition to the national parks, throughout Spain there are more than a score of areas where man's activities are restricted to, say, controlled forestry and certain grazing. They draw hundreds of thousands of visitors each year, not all of them tidy.*

*Other "natural parts" have been set aside for biological research. Madrid and Barcelona districts have taken the lead in the concept of hospital centres, manned by volunteers, for the treatment and rehabilitation of sick or injured wild creatures. The work is gaining ground, and is allied to the principle of captive breeding of sorely endangered species, for later release into their natural environment.*

*"Restoring fauna is not simply a question of preserving the biotypes and saving them from pollution," wrote zoologist Dr Michel Fernex. "It also entails re-establishing the balance of nature by progressively reintroducing species which have disappeared through various causes."*

*Returning captive-bred species to their habitats appears to be no easy task. Yet where successful, Dr Fernex declares in ringing* tones, "it can be compared with the restoration of a cathedral."

Early in the Eighties, Spain signed the Berne Convention on conserving wildlife and habitats such as mountains and wetlands, and later joined the International Union for the Conservation of Nature. The country's entry into the European Common Market meant acceptance of that body's laws, present and future, concerning protection of the environment, outlawing, among other aspects, the killing of rare fauna, and land and sea pollution.

David Baird, a journalist with many years' experience of both rural and urban Spain, states: "Clashes between agronomists, industrialists, politicians, farmers and ecologists will continue. But a new national awareness of the need for environmental protection is evidenced by the growth of ecological pressure groups.

"The battle is no longer as one-sided as it was."

Particularly promising is the fact that, as a result of classroom instruction and conservation campaigns, Spanish children — once notorious for stoning or baiting any animal that moved, and for tearing down birds' nests "for fun" — are now excitedly identifying wild animals and birds of their country, and learning their ways of life.

Increasing tens of thousands of youngsters appreciate the value and importance of conservation through TV features and books, or first-hand contacts with wild species in the reserves. Some children have got together to form wildlife clubs.

Hundreds of ecological pressure groups, consisting chiefly of men and women in their mid-twenties and thirties, number among the enemies of wildlife those bureaucrats out to exploit and profit from natural resources. They are being fought strenuously, and the groups are growing in number. Their work, together with the creation of nature sanctuaries and increased official and public awareness of the difficulties facing some specimens, has had a positive effect on wildlife.

Spain has set an example in the protection of fauna that might well be followed by other countries, and the move represents a milestone in Madrid's conservation campaigns. A special force of a thousand members of the Guardia Civil, in other times and respects not the most popular of police organizations, is at work throughout the country monitoring and controlling "all anti-nature activities." The men trained for this service have special powers, particularly in protecting species in danger of extinction.

So the popular conception of the average Spaniard as indifferent to the welfare of wild beings needs revising. And the days when only beasts that fought in the bullring aroused interest are passing. Orchestrated by zoologists, biologists, ecologists, ornithologists, naturalists and nature-lovers, there's a novel national awareness, led by King Juan Carlos, of the need for environmental concern.

*E. R.*

# CHAPTER ONE

# The Spanish

# Leopard

THERE was no sound. But some instinct of danger made me look up. Ears laid back, amber eyes glowing, the big wild cat stared down at me from the fork of a solitary pine. Its golden, spotted coat rippling, the animal gave a wide-mouthed, hissing snarl.

Less than a dozen feet from my head was a leopard in miniature.

Fearing that it was about to spring, I stepped back swiftly, then glanced up again. The animal, a yard long from head to tail, had vanished like some tawny apparition into the sandy scrubland of tangled heather, blackberry bushes, small blue irises, and juniper clumps.

After many long days on the trail, I had at last caught a glimpse, thrilling and unforgettable, of the rare and elusive Spanish lynx *(Lynx pardina)*, high on the list of the world's endangered species.

My brief encounter with this handsome wild animal took place in Doñana national park. I had toured the park's savannah, sand dunes and the vast marshlands of the Guadalquivir estuary with a world authority on the creature, Dr Miguel Delibes Jr., son of the well-known Spanish novelist, naturalist and hunter.

Dr Delibes' field studies over many years, sparked off by his father's strong interest in nature, have led him and other scientists to the conclusion that there may be now "only a few hundred" Spanish lynx surviving in the country, principally in the hills and mountains of central and southern Spain.

Dr Delibes and others in the small coterie of lynx-watchers can't be more specific about Spain's lynx population because of its sparse, widely-scattered numbers and its wraith-like elusiveness. There are, however, encouraging reports of the creature being glimpsed in some parts where this feline had not been seen for decades. Naturalists were jubilant when one was photographed in December 1985, only 20 miles from the centre of Madrid.

Such sightings are highly prized by experts. Miguel Delibes won recognition as a leading authority on the lynx at a pan-European wildlife conference in Strasburg some years ago. Delegates from over a dozen countries stood up one by one and told of odd sightings. Others admitted they had never seen any species of the animal. Prolonged applause was accorded to the Spanish biologist when he reported having logged some 30 fleeting meetings with *Lynx pardina* in various parts of his country, as a result of years of

*A Spanish lynx, with its prey, a partridge. An expert hunter, the lynx is one of the country's rarest animals.*

careful and patient tracking.

"Wild cats around the world — from the cheetah in Africa to America's bobcat and the Asian caracal — have long been persecuted by man," said Dr Delibes as we trekked over the rough, bushy terrain in Doñana. "Our beautiful lynx is no exception. It does not attack man. It's the other way round."

Throughout the day, we examined deep claw-lines of the big cats on the gnarled trunks of oak trees. Or knelt in the burning sand to peer at lynx spoor.

Finally, we surveyed the ravaged bracken of a bloody midnight skirmish. There I learned the story of a young rabbit doe's end (killed by a single bite at the neck was Dr Delibes' assessment) from shards of bone and undigested fur he picked out from a dried lynx dropping. The attacker had crept up to within five yards of its victim, remaining as immobile as a rock. When the rabbit raised its head, the lynx shot out and leapt on the doe with all the force of a powerful spring.

As my guide read the signs at the scene of each new discovery, a picture slowly emerged, like a developing photographic print, of this fascinating carnivore.

NO one, I soon realized, could ever confuse the Spanish lynx — at around 30 lb. smaller but more regally speckled than its first cousin, the dwindling European lynx — with, say, a tigerish tom-cat. For one thing, it's several times heavier than the domestic animal.

The undisputed king of Iberia's wild felines, with only humans and the odd wolf as enemies, *Lynx pardina* pounces on its prey with the short, lethal dash of a leopard (whose spotted fur its coat resembles). So lithe as to appear boneless, this audacious prowler of the night, dawn and dusk is an expert swimmer and climber, and possesses ultrasensitive sight with which it can pick out its supper in the pitch darkness of a moonless night.

Although it has a relatively weak sense of smell, the cat's large, tapering ears are topped with tufts of black hair that act as antennae, sensitive to air currents during up-wind stalking and to the slightest rustle in the undergrowth. With these the lynx can monitor sounds inaudible to the human ear, and is able to slip into hiding minutes before an approaching human being comes into view.

Strong, padded paws, a coral-red tongue, a surprisingly short tail, exploratory white whiskers, those steadfast, fiery eyes and a coat of mottled ochre — a perfect disguise that merges with sun-dappled vegetation — complete the picture.

As we wandered among the stunted bushes, Dr Delibes said he had to search many months before he saw his first lynx.

"Then one day I came across a magnificent specimen stretched out, fast asleep, on a limb of a cork-oak. Breathing deeply and twitching his ears now and then to ward off the flies buzzing around him, he filled the eye-pieces of my binoculars. The magic moment I had dreamed about for so long had come true."

Another time, parking his open safari vehicle under an umbrella pine, he disturbed a fully-grown female sprawled out in the branches after a night's hunting.

"Suddenly, she leapt out — several feet in the air and right over the bonnet of the Jeep. I was scared she would attack me. But she dashed into the vegetation and disappeared."

Dr Delibes says stories about the lynx springing on its quarry from a tree are largely untrue. It seems they invariably hunt by territorial stalking, sometimes covering five or six miles at an easy lope.

"As a rule, they only climb trees in the daytime. And then only to snooze in peace."

A lynx's home range might be four or five square miles, marked here and there by their strong-smelling urine to warn off other feline hunters. Able to travel long distances to settle in new regions, their exceptional adaptability gives rise to hopes that their numbers might increase.

In the worst days of winter when its coverts are wet or under snow, the lynx as a matter of survival remains active, leaving its thick scrub to hunt in open territory, at any hour of the day.

I T'S thought that in the Ice Ages the animal now known as *pardina* was found in large numbers throughout European forests, co-existing on overlapping ranges with the larger but less striking European species now confined to isolated areas in the north and east of the Continent.

One species of the lynx family was active at the time of New Stone Age Man and inhabited Britain, including the region where London now stands. But the primitives clubbed them to extinction for the animals' fine skins, which they used as warm clothing.

In its halcyon days the Spanish lynx inhabited all the country's mountain ranges and foothills from the Pyrenees to the Atlantic coast. The sharp decline of the species began in the early days of this century with the progressive replacement of goat-herding by the cultivation of wheat and other cereals. Because of the ensuing farmers' wars on rabbits the lynx was deprived of much of its staple food. An average-sized rabbit provides little more than a day's supply of food for an adult lynx.

The animal was also the target of unrestrained hunting over many years in the belief that it was necessary to kill predators in order to protect other fauna. From the mid-Fifties to the Sixties, the lynx's numbers sank even further when myxomatosis eliminated millions of rabbits in Spain.

Although now strictly protected by law, Spanish lynx are feared lost every year, killed in farmers' or poachers' traps, or shot illegally by trophy hunters. With a feline's inquisitiveness regarding strange objects, the lynx will attempt to play with any new discovery. When this turns out to be a trap it becomes a

*Caught here in mid leap, the Spanish Lynx hunts by pouncing on its prey with a short, lethal dash.*

classic but mournful example of curiosity killing the cat.

Or a lynx might try to take a rabbit from such a trap and be caught in another nearby. With its legs mangled by the steel jaws, the injured animal is killed as an act of mercy, perhaps, by the farmer who, incidentally, is left with a rare pelt worth tens of thousands of pesetas.

Over the last two decades, the Spanish government has accepted responsibility for the preservation of *pardina*. However, because a lynx will in isolated incidents raid a chicken house or seize a lamb, many small farmers still regard it as vermin, a fleeting menace to be trapped, poisoned, or shot on sight.

Government officials admit the animal's alleged depredations are still used as an excuse by some farmers and hunters for slaughtering it. The farmers want to get the lynx off their lands; the hunters want pelts which bring rich rewards on the black market.

There's a fine of several thousands of pounds or a gaol sentence for illegally hunting or deliberately trapping a lynx. And there's financial compensation for anyone who can substantiate a claim that his livestock has been savaged by it.

Naturalists maintain the government's protection measures are not enough to guard against this hunter being hunted for its regal coat to make, say, a bolero, a bedside rug or a horseman's saddle-cloth. A coat of a dozen or so pelts smuggled out of the country will fetch up to £25,000 in Paris, a situation which caused an embittered conservationist to remark to me: "The only lynx we might see today is on some wealthy woman's back."

Also affecting the fate of the lynx is the continued cutting down of indigenous forests to make way for the planting of fast-growing eucalyptus trees for the paper and timber industries. The lynx's normal habitats are being destroyed by the vast timberland processes. And it's forced to wander elsewhere. An ally has appeared in the unlikely form of the small farmer, engaged in a country-wide eucalyptus war. Tens of thousands of the young immigrant gum, or eucalyptus, trees which at maturity burn out the soil and ravage the ecology have been regularly uprooted at night by villagers, whose traditional ways of existence are at stake.

Yet another factor keeping the lynx numbers low is its comparatively poor reproduction rate.

Heralded by shrill and prolonged caterwauling like any cat on the roof-tiles, lynx courtships begin when in midwinter the female is on heat.

After 63–73 days' gestation, a litter of blind but fully-furred and endearing kittens is born in an underground burrow strewn with grass and leaves or, perhaps, in a den among rocks, in the heart

*The author Eric Robins (left) with lynx expert Dr Miguel Delibes in the Coto de Doñana in southern Spain.*

of a bramble bush. Or the hollow trunk of a dead cork-oak. Parents have been known to use an abandoned storks' nest set on the upper branches of a tree.

Generally, there are two or three kittens. If there are four or more, they will probably be weaklings doomed to die. The mother finds it too difficult these days to feed such a number. One rabbit might just about satisfy a couple of youngsters, but at least three rabbits would have to be caught every day to feed four or more of them.

And, whatever the number, the kittens are always guests. The mother, as a provider, is genetically the most important member of the family, so the young are obliged to wait until she has eaten her fill.

"I've watched a female slap back her kittens from a dead goose with bared claws as sharp as sailcloth needles," said Dr Delibes. "I've seen her devour a whole rabbit while her little family looked on, mewing with hunger."

Instinctively, the mother is building up, or preserving, her strength so she can keep on ranging far and wide in search of prey to feed them all. Her own energy needs may at times compel her to eat a kill without returning to the den. In this way, a trio of undernourished offspring become vulnerable to fatal diseases.

Facing a lifetime of from 10 to 20 years, the young lynx first practise stalking each other much like the kittens of house-cats. Out of the den, they soon pick up the hunting techniques. While stalking and pouncing are instinctive, these moves must be practised under the mother's eye.

They are taught how to inflict a swift, mortal bite, killing the prey promptly despite its struggles. They catch their first prey, perhaps a rat or a mouse, at four to five months, and are independent soon afterwards. The young become highly accomplished predators like their parents, moving swiftly and silently through the undergrowth with shoulders hunched and body flattened.

Dr Juan Antonio Fernández, a Spanish naturalist and author, recounts the drama of a fully-grown female swimming marsh-pools to snatch a greylag goose whose companions had ignored magpies scolding overhead, warning of the lynx's approach.

"She stretched low through the sedge," wrote Dr Fernández. "Her legendary vision was concentrated on the big geese, selecting a victim. A sudden burst of speed and a bound through the vegetation ended in a resounding impact and a cloud of feathers from a slashed breast. A frantic wrestling match ensued before the doomed bird was subdued."

Lynx have been seen carrying young wild boar in their mouths, and there's a record of the killing of a fallow deer doe and three fawns by lynx springing at their jugular veins. After a headlong dash, a pair of lynx can drag down and kill an adult stag.

Dr Delibes told me the lynx's hunting techniques are those of "an evolved feline" with specialized "rules" of conduct for killing small prey (a bite in the neck or the nape of the neck) and large prey (a bite in the throat).

A black legend associated with the lynx is that now and again it kills fawns merely to exercise its hunting prowess. Observers' opinions vary on whether or not the animal may kill for the sake of killing.

Giving rise to stories of wanton mercilessness is the fact that only the shoulders, rump, legs or head of a deer may be eaten. Then, the animal's pangs surfeited, the rest of the carcass is abandoned.

Miguel Delibes admits large prey such as adult red or fallow deer are sometimes attacked. He insists this is because of hunger, and not just a cruel exercise.

It's clear the Spanish lynx remains tragically vulnerable. What can be done to save it from oblivion?

Unfortunately, it has been found that, as a rule, lynx won't mate and breed in captivity to help bolster the line. Kittens reared artificially sicken and die slowly. So specialists have urged stricter control of land-clearing and commercial deforestation; the banning in lynx areas of snares and poisons put down for foxes, genets and crows; and the creation and control of more rabbit-breeding territories.

There has already been an official response to one of these demands. New grasslands and pine groves where the rabbit populations can increase and provide more food — more readily — for the lynx are being established.

In Doñana, the last figure given for the lynx population was 40. Apart from the animal's low-level rate of reproduction affecting its numbers, there have been several recent tragedies within the environs of the park alone. Some have died in snares outside its boundaries. One was killed by a car on a road skirting the reserve. Another adult drowned in an uncovered well on surrounding irrigated land.

A bronze sculpture of the Spanish lynx stands on a dusty access road to Doñana, and the setting sun throws this replica into sharp relief. Let's hope the time will never come when this singular feline is swallowed up for ever — leaving behind in the countryside only a cold shell of weathered metal as a reminder such a proud and noble animal once lived here.

# CHAPTER TWO

# A Royal Bird's

# Battle

WITH a silhouette similar to the golden eagle's, the Spanish imperial eagle is the westernmost survivor of a species once common in Mongolia, the steppes of Siberia, north-west India, the Balkans, North Africa and a large part of Europe.

Its fierce, haughty profile appeared on the coats of arms of Spanish nobility from the 16th century.

Today the imperial eagle *(Aquila heliaca adalberti)* is one of the rarest birds in the skies. Its continued existence is in the hands of the Spanish people who are, at last, rediscovering it as a national emblem.

It may not be beyond recall, but so precarious has the imperial

*The imperilled Imperial Eagle, once widespread throughout Spain, now survives in a few isolated pockets*

eagle's lifeline become at the hands of man it's estimated only 130 pairs remain alive. Their stronghold is Spain: Andalusia, the Pyrenees, the mountain territory of Cantabria, the lordly sierras of Castile and similar highlands.

The Spanish imperial eagle is now a separate entity of the original breed, with its own distinctive colouration — chocolate-brown plumage with bold, white shoulder patches — blending perfectly with its restricted habitats.

The present sparse population stems from a turn-of-the-century invasion of the Iberian peninsula by legions of trophy hunters from central Europe whose shotguns blasted away at the birds in a cruel and heedless fashion. The full extent of the massacre over the years is unknown. But one example of it is on record: on a single day in one small, Spanish rural area, 23 adult imperials were shot down. Rising from large nests on low-growing trees, they were particularly subject to slaughter.

In 1952 an epidemic of myxomatosis throughout the country brought further misfortune to the birds. The disease took a heavy toll on the rabbit population, effectively depriving the eagles of their staple food. Forced to change their way of life and regular diet, they took to hunting such unusual prey as magpies and ducks, snakes and lizards, even fish and puppy-dogs. The rabbit famine was as near-mortal a blow to the species as the hunter's rampages.

Urban development took its toll as well. Twenty per cent of the remaining pairs disappeared in a quarter of a century from 1960. The birds are ultra-sensitive to human approach. In the populated Madrid region in 1987, when house and road building led to the loss of their forest habitats, 40 per cent of the couples were forced to retreat.

In olden times, the imperial eagles nested in the majority of Spain's mountain ranges and hills. Today they might be glimpsed among some mountain slopes not too precipitous nor tangled with vegetation. There will be within range umbrella pines and cork-oaks, ilex meadows and plains with rabbit colonies.

Importantly, more than a dozen breeding pairs — slowly increasing — live in safety and freedom in Coto Doñana by an Atlantic shore. There were only seven nests there 20 years ago, but two more a decade later. It's to be hoped the Doñana breeds are slowly but surely holding their own.

O N a recent day-long visit to this great sanctuary, I climbed a 20-foot-high wooden observation tower overlooking one of the nests, and came face to face with

a mature female feeding a couple of gawky youngsters with scraps of a hare her mate had left dangling in a neighbouring oak.

Apart from clicking her powerful beak in warning as she looked up briefly from her ministrations to fix me with an imperious stare, she gave no sign of resenting my intrusion into her domestic life. Despite a savage appearance and that baleful glance, she seemed in those surroundings to possess an urbane, almost amiable, temperament.

A question often asked of the guards: what happens to young eagles prospecting outside the park? Food (which is life) dictates the habits of the birds and other creatures, and the quantity and variety of this within the protected area of Doñana invariably brings them back home.

"The eagles sense they are safe here," a government biologist studying in Doñana told me. "They have become relatively tame."

Like many of his colleagues, he was angry with people who still look on eagles as "harmful," regarded as vermin preying on domestic stock.

"The reverse is true," he said. "Eagles are good friends of man, especially the small farmer. They keep down such crop-eating pests as rabbits and rodents, helping to maintain nature's balance."

Hazards still faced by the imperial eagle outside such havens as Doñana include odd cases of illegal shooting (despite increasingly heavy penalties); the wilful destruction of nests by peasants who regard birds of prey as rivals for the rabbits they kill for the cook-pot; the putting down of poisoned baits for wolves, foxes and rats;

*Previous pages: watched by a chick, an Imperial Eagle homes in with another twig for its nest. The nests grow larger every year with continued use.*

wire snares; radioactive waste in rivers, agricultural and industrial pollutants. The high residue of toxic chemicals found in abandoned eggs represents a chilling, comparatively new, threat to breeding.

There have been cases, too, of imperial eagles electrocuted by power lines intersecting the countryside.

Some threats derive from the habits of the bird itself. Their large nests of branches, twigs, dried grass and ferns that grow bigger every year as new woodland materials are added measure a yard or more across and at the top of a tree are visible from far away. They are easy targets for self-styled sportsmen and egg poachers who command high prices running into hundreds of pounds for eggs of such rare and wonderful birds.

The eggs which escape being seized produce a plump and engaging ball of white fluff, weighing over a pound at birth.

The mother stays continually on guard over the newly-hatched chicks — usually two, and rarely these days more than three. When the male has flown off in search of food, she remains with her strong wings folded round the chicks like a cloak.

As I saw in that Doñana nest, at a very early age the eaglets instinctively claw and bite twigs in mock killings. After about 40 days, when the young are large enough to be left for spells, both parents go out on hunting forays to satisfy the appetites of their ever-hungry offspring.

When they are two months old, the young eagles, now completely covered in cinnamon-brown feathers, begin their apprenticeship. Attacking imaginary prey, they learn all the intricate techniques of soaring flight from parents who lead them onward and upward. A series of impetuous and daring pirouettes follows.

The adults start their daily task of scanning the plains from the sky at sunrise. They work regular hours to a biological time-clock which governs the eating, drinking, sleeping and sexual behaviour of animals.

In the mornings they hunt until about 11, and in summer evenings after five.

I watched a pair at work one morning in the heart of Spain. With sharp, barking cries of "Owk, owk," wings extended to a six-foot span, they circled the sun-dappled fields.

Suddenly, they saw the flicker of a white bob-tail by a meandering stream far below. The male bird swooped, and in a deadly split-second seized a young buck-rabbit.

Clutching the kill in its claws, followed by its mate, the eagle flew off. Somewhere over the horizon there was a bulky, ramshackle nest in a gnarled tree where rapacious chicks were crying for yet another meal.

But should there have been no luck during the morning hunt, the male stays alert. Perched motionless on top of a tall tree or rocky outcrop, he sweeps the countryside with binocular vision, or watches a quarry until it can be surprised and attacked in a clearing.

There are ornithologists who think the Spanish imperial eagle lacks the verve and skills of other large raptors. But the imperial is scarcely lazy, and has a good deal of intelligence and cunning when required.

At times, even large birds of almost their own weight are tackled by a pair cleverly using a technique that relies on the victim being gregarious. For instance, bird-watchers have reported seeing a male imperial flushing a gaggle of greylag geese from a clump of reeds by zooming low over them, its wings casting a swift-moving and sinister shadow. The female then dived to scatter the bunched birds — and the male snatched up a plump goose that in the panic had become separated from its companions.

The well-known American author, James A. Michener, in his monumental *Iberia* describes a variation of the smart hunting

*An Imperial Eagle with two youngsters. When they are two months old, they are ready to learn to fly.*

tactics of "these noblest of birds," in Doñana.

"No eagle flying alone has ever been seen to take a goose except by sheer accident," he says. "Although the eagle is stronger and has powerful talons, he cannot overtake a goose in full flight; pursuit is useless. Therefore the eagle finds himself a partner, and as a pair they become formidable.

"One flies rather high, in the fly-space of the goose, and somewhat awkwardly so that the target gets the idea that he can outfly this enemy. The other eagle flies low and well behind the first, and as the 'awkward' eagle maintains an altitude on the goose and makes a series of futile passes at him, the big bird takes the easy way out and with adept spirals evades the eagle by dropping to a lower altitude, where the second eagle sweeps in with terrifying talons."

OVER a natural reserve on the river Tajo, another comparative refuge for *Aquila heliaca adalberti,* I was fortunate to see what all scientific observers and patient bird-watchers long to experience — the spectacular nuptial display of a pair of imperial eagles some five or six years old.

For three hours I had waited on a grassy knoll under a brazen noonday sun. Then I heard harsh, excited cries.

Two large bird-shapes appeared in the cloudless sky and began a series of elegant circlings, wings and pinion feathers outstretched. I watched them through night-glasses.

After they had soared together for a few minutes, one bird took the initiative and dived at its chosen mate. As if playing tag, both male and female took part in an uninhibited display of aerial swoops and chases. Finally, one bird rolled on its back in mid-air and presented its unsheathed talons to the other. Interlocked, the pair came whirling down hundreds of feet before levelling out and flying apart over my head.

British naturalist and Fellow of the Royal Geographical Society, Douglas Botting, describes these fantastic mating gyrations as "a superb example" of bird flight.

Young Marcos Rodríguez Pantoja, however, had a much closer and enduring relationship with imperial eagles. As a seven-year-old, Marcos was abandoned for 12 years with a herd of goats in a remote valley of the Sierra Morena in south-west Spain. During his strange, magical childhood, he became a friend of the imperial eagles and other animals and birds for, in a cloak of skins, he was as wild as his winged and four-footed companions.

Brought back to civilization, he told Dr Gabriel Janer Manila, a University of Palma psychologist, of his life and adventures with the birds.

"One day I climbed an oak tree to see an eagles' nest," Marcos told him. "I took a rabbit and tied it to my waist and climbed the oak tree where the eagles' nest was, and when I was getting near the nest the eagles thought I was going to take their young away from them.

"So they grabbed my hair in their claws, and I grabbed a branch and hit them with the branch. And they watched what I was doing. I took the rabbit and started to feed it to the little ones, and they [the parents] made as if they were going to charge at me. But seeing I was feeding their children they stopped bothering me."

Marcos tells of a missing goat kid. The herd had left it behind, asleep.

"I couldn't find him anywhere and I was calling away when an eagle came and started to jump in front of me. He'd begin to fly and then stop, then he went on ahead and jumped on the kid and woke it up, and the kid went 'baa, baa, baa!' when he saw the eagle close."

But the eagles did not attack goats "because they had a lot of small prey like partridges and rabbits."

Marcos adds: "This was at nightfall. I took the kid in my arms, and I patted the eagle, and kissed her, and she went away happy.

"When the eagles caught a rabbit or partridge they brought it to me so I'd cut it up for them. They'd go at it with their claws and their beaks and break it up... Another day I was making a fire so I could catch a rabbit and roast it, and an eagle who'd been watching me showed up with a rabbit.

"I thought it was for me but when she saw I was cutting it up in order to roast it, she started staring at me — like this — and started to go 'gro, gro.' I didn't know what she wanted to tell me. She flew off and brought me a partridge, so I cut it up for her; she took one piece in her beak, and one in each claw; she took three pieces."

AN imperial eagle would be a rare sight over the Sierra Morena these days, a reminder that nature's doomsday clock stands at a few minutes to midnight for one of our most glorious birds of prey.

The imperial eagle is immensely powerful and impressive, but it's desperately vulnerable too. If actions to sustain and foster the birds are not maintained, future generations will never have the chance to experience those thrilling, age-old rituals of hunting and mating I had witnessed from lonely rural viewpoints.

Children will only know *Aquila* in illustrated books like this, in museums or television playbacks.

# CHAPTER THREE

# The Gentle Wolf

SUPERSTITIOUS country people who still believe in werewolves fear the animal as an evil creature of the night whose eerie howl is a portent of tragedy. Lonely travellers in forests of the hinterland cross themselves and mutter prayers to the saints to protect them from the dreaded *hombre lobo.*

So ingrained are these beliefs, in some parts of northern Spain there have been incidents of captured or wounded wolves being sadistically tortured by peasants before the victims were put to death.

It's a distressing picture because to well-known scientists like Ramón Grande del Brio, who have made close and exhaustive

studies of the species, the Big Bad Wolf syndrome is nonsense.

Take the Spanish wolf. Slightly smaller than its timber wolf brethren of northern Europe, it is a sociable and intelligent animal — safer, in fact, than many pet dogs like, say, some Rottweilers or bull-terriers. But it has long suffered from a reputation as a vicious killer of livestock and, accordingly, has been endlessly pursued as an enemy by rural folk using high-powered rifles or shotguns. Shootings are supplemented with poisoned baits and steel-jawed traps that inflict ghastly injuries.

Forest fires and the cutting down of pine woods and oak groves to plant fast-growing alien trees for newsprint and cellulose add to their troubles.

Dedicated long-term researchers who have literally, and seemingly fearlessly, laid down with a pack of wolves report having been merely licked tenderly, or sniffed at as "just another creature." Yet from the Middle Ages, despite the saga of Romulus and Remus, the founders of Rome said to have been suckled by a she-wolf, *Lobo ibérico* and its kin have been regarded by the ignorant of many eras as a harbinger of the devil, savaging men and women or carrying off children in slavering jaws. Modern horror films and TV shock-shows have perpetuated the myth.

The more realistic view of this hunting carnivore is that it preys on kid-goats or sheep and raids hen coops only because of its increasingly desperate situation and the need to feed a family and itself.

Whatever the roots of prejudice, research shows the wolf not as the ruthless creature of popular belief but as an affectionate wild animal devoted to the care of its offspring and living within orderly societies of well-established relationships.

*Agile and mysterious, a Spanish Wolf on the move. The wolf is a social animal that lives within a complex hierarchy.*

Wolves are commonly associated in people's minds with shadowy forests at night. They have been driven there, however, by men and, in many instances, have had to abandon their traditional, daylight stalking of deer and other wild prey in open country.

Wolves need space. Where possible wolves establish pre-determined, circular habitats — territories within territories. The vixen and cubs occupy the inner circle; the second area is where the young males and their older relatives meet, and the third, largest territory is where the senior males hunt for food. These sometimes bring back prey half-alive to the cubs to teach them how to defend themselves and subdue a kill. The youngsters will play with a fox carcass for hours, "killing" it several times over before tiring of the game.

Within the three-dimensional habitat the oldest dominant male or pack leader is well respected. Any younger contender has to wait until the doyen dies before he can take over.

Wolf groups have a complicated body language. They can look quite different to each other, as individual domestic animals do to those familiar with them.

Ancestor of the domestic dog, to us the wolf looks like a large, lean German shepherd, with slanting eyes. Many of the habits of dogs, such as tail-wagging, have their origins within the social organization of the wolf-pack. With domestic dogs, the human family becomes the pack and the owner takes the place of the dominant male. In the hierarchy, the dominant wolf shows its authority by holding its head high and tail erect.

A wolf trying to establish a higher-ranking position may initiate a challenge by staring at an older animal, maintaining eye contact. Such a provocative signal can lead to an aggressive leap by the challenged wolf as it tries to enforce its dominance.

Growling, lip-curling, showing teeth and pointing the ears back (all actions inherited by dogs) are the signs used by a wolf

*Two wolves survey the countryside from a safe perch. They are a protected species in some parts of Spain, but are persecuted in others.*

that feels threatened as when, for example, another might try tosteal its food. And the warning can include a sharp snap.

Wolves will also bark in defence of their dens, usually a natural crevice or the abandoned den of a fox or badger.

Submissiveness, as in a dog, is signalled by flattened ears and tail between the legs.

And tail-wagging, of course, is a greeting.

The wolf's blood-curdling, mournful howl is used to keep in contact with other members of the pack or to advertise its presence to other packs, warning them to keep away.

Where possible, wolves hunt deer and other ungulates,

especially in winter, but will also take rodents and ground-birds. When the wolves have eaten their fill, they cache the remains, using front paws (again like a dog) to scrape a hole in the ground and noses to shovel back the earth.

The gentle side of the Spanish wolf is vividly illustrated by Marcos Rodríguez, the former wild boy of the Sierra Morena.

There he had become friendly with a family of wolves to whom he took meat from a slaughtered deer, in a sack.

"The parents would stop me, but once they saw I came to feed them [the cubs] they began to trust me. I smelled like them.

"Once I picked up one of the cubs and by mistake I hurt it a little and the she-wolf right next to me struck at me with her claws. But we knew each other well.

"I needed them when I saw I was in danger, or I had lost my way. I would start howling 'Ooooooo' (then I could do it better), and some wolves would come to me since they knew I fed them and their children. Well, they saw I didn't know my way, it was a really high forest. I cried and they jumped up at me and grabbed my arms in their mouths till I laughed; then they showed me the way to their cave, the den, and from there I knew the way."

The cubs were Marcos's playmates.

"Whenever I went there all the cubs would be waiting, and they would begin to play and jump up and down."

At no time did the wolves of the sierra attack the boy's goats.

But when one of the herd died, Marcos would start to howl "and the wolves would come and eat it."

MARCOS's little friends the wolfcubs were inquisitive, ever-hungry fur-balls.

At five weeks each would have weighed about 15 lb. A fortnight later, they'd venture short distances with adults. For wolves, the young — communally fed, reared and defended — are the centre of the universe.

Generally, males and females in a pack form a dominant social order, and it's the higher-ranking animals that breed. Most members of a pack are related.

Some of the youngsters might stay with a pack for as long as four years, possibly longer, sometimes rearing cubs themselves. Normally, one of the females has cubs each year.

Feeding rapidly-growing young puts heavy pressure on the talents and stamina of the providers, who are inclined to follow a pack routine such as:

1. After hunting, 12 hours' sleep.
2. Bouts of play and social interaction, up to two hours.
3. A daily hunt by most of the mature males.
4. Feeding the cubs. Ears back, these crouch and lick rapidly the mouth of the adult that regurgitates partly-digested food. Later in life, the clamouring cubs will be fed chunks of meat from a cache, or given bones and even young rabbits.

Each cub is born with an instinctive assertiveness. Adults rehearse this with them, gently pinning down each son or daughter, as part of possessive play, forcing them to lie still with their necks to the ground. The cubs then practise this routine on each other.

Play-acting allows each youngster to test and hone its competitive skills and the basic aggressive, selfish spirit lurking beneath the skin of every living thing, allied to survival.

ONE of the difficulties of protecting the wolf, forced by adverse circumstances to range wider and wider for its livelihood, is that it does not recognize political boundaries. And policies towards the controversial wolf vary according to the politics of the local authorities.

Some socialistic outlooks appear to be more tolerant and understanding of the wolf than those of right-wing bodies. But attempts to safeguard the animal are not helped when, of

*Wolves, including this one killed in a hunt in 1948, are still considered a serious menace to livestock by many country folk.*

necessity, it wanders into provinces where, as a member of one of Spain's ecological organizations put it, "it is at the mercy of anyone with a grudge and a gun."

When the townspeople of Potes in Cantabria, 45 miles southwest of Santander, met to discuss the activities of wolves in parts of the north and west — hungry packs in at least three areas were said to have killed domestic animals including two horses — local farmers angrily shrugged off claims that the stomach contents of dead wolves had shown wild animals to have been a larger part of their diet than domestic stock; rejected the proposition of officially-supervised hunting parties, and continually shouted, "Kill the lot."

Commendably, Andalusia has given a lead to other regions by striking the wolf from the list of wild animals that may be hunted. There's now a heavy fine for killing one, and shepherds are well compensated for any losses proved to have been caused by wolves.

The measure may be only just in time. Marcos's companions of a few years ago have shrunk in number to about 20 survivors. It's estimated there are no more than a few hundred wolves in the entire country — in Galicia, the northern mountains, Zamora and Leon. While Andalusia has taken a late step welcomed by conservationists, other districts — like Cantabria, where it isregarded as "an agricultural pest" — have put a bounty on the wolf's head. There are authorized wolf-shooting parties where beaters drive the animals on to the guns and scores of ravening dogs. Another heartless form of so-called wolf-control is to poison the cubs in their dens.

Since the late president of the United States, big-game hunter Theodore Roosevelt, hand on the Bible, swore to exterminate the wolf, ideas about wild animals have changed. But for the wolf not that much.

Keen hunters, vociferously defensive of their right to the "sport" of random killing, are still numerous. So wolves, focus of fear, hostility, superstition and monumental ignorance, are a dwindling species.

Centuries have passed since the Celts revered the wolf as sacred. Its first modern defender was Farley Mowat, a talented Canadian biologist. In 1963, after closely observing the daily life of a family headed by devoted parents he called "George" and "Angelina," he exploded the myths of the wolf as a cruel and treacherous animal. His verdict: "A palpable lie."

Watching adults share in the care and upbringing of the young, Mowat noted a wolf he called "Uncle Albert" was "a splendid babysitter." He established that, unlike *Homo sapiens,* the wolf never kills for fun. Nor takes more than it and the family can use.

During his long research in the wild, Mowat found that often the wolves' hunting was unsuccessful; and the super-killer image collapsed when at one period he observed the wolves living largely on mice.

Major studies followed — by, among others, American biologist David Hech, Dutch mammalogist Dr J. van Haaften and Spain's Del Brio. All confirmed the wolf's peaceable image and revealed more of the animal's sense of territory, social organization and behaviour, and its devoted family life.

They discovered the wolf's communications system uses all five senses and is as precise as a computerized print-out. It seems stance, body contact, scent-marking, widely-assorted vocalizing (in cubs, the howling is a distress signal for food) are instant indicators of some situation or another.

Such research exposed another fallacy — of the wolf as a threat to man. In fact and in legend, rabid animals have brought terror and death. But not a single instance was authenticated by these and other scientists of a deliberate attack on human beings by a healthy wolf.

With the wolf declared largely innocent and rabies now rare, guilt falls mainly on feral dogs and dog-wolf hybrids. Wandering wild and hungry, such animals are the greater menace to domestic flocks. But few shepherds will admit it since "wolf damage" might bring official compensation.

Middle-aged biologists Manuel Pereira and his wife Rute studied the Iberian sub-species of wolf in relation to humans and a prey species, the roe deer. The couple raised three wolfcubs, two males and a female, brought to them by shepherds who had come upon them alone in a den. The cubs soon saw the Pereiras as parents.

"They behaved as in a normal wolf family — submissively to Manuel, the dominant male," says Rute. "And all three responded to me as their firm and affectionate mother."

An anthropologist who heads a campaign to save the wolf says there are alternatives to indiscriminate attempts at extermination.

"The wolf," he believes, "is a noble animal, too long

*Wolf-cubs raised by humans follow their surrogate "pack leader" on a run through the country.*

misunderstood."

Yet he reluctantly accepts that legal hunting, properly organized and controlled, might have to continue as part of the conservation campaign. His argument: legal hunting lessens poaching, the use of cruelly-maiming snares and the putting down of food-baits injected with strychnine.

Scattered and isolated, it becomes harder each year for the wolves to find an ecosystem — those "nurseries of new-life forms" — where they can mate, breed and successfully rear their cubs. In many countries, more wolves are killed annually than are born.

Like most endangered species, the wolf's future depends on man's ability, or otherwise, to co-exist with the natural world. International co-operation within the EEC in interbreeding may be the only way to save the animal which, as wolf-watcher Adolph Murie wrote in the Forties, "typifies the wilderness so completely."

A handful of scientists and naturalists in Spain, Portugal and other parts of Europe have banded together in a Wolf Group — *Grupo Lobo* — that runs an education and propaganda campaign on behalf of the creature. Members have been encouraged by the fact that schoolchildren, at least, have shown through their essays, poems and drawings, they want the wolf to win. Associations of animal-lovers in Asturias and Galicia are continuing their campaigns in defence of the wolf.

Polls taken by Spanish magazines devoted to nature have shown that in urban areas of the country the wolf shares with the brown bear and the lynx the accolade of "the most popular wild animals."

Country people questioned were less enthusiastic. Many of them named the wolf, along with foxes, vipers and hedgehogs, among the most detested Iberian fauna.

Led by Spain, special attention has now been given to the conservation of the wolf in Europe. A Spanish scientist collated reports within his own country and from Portugal, Italy and Greece (the only countries within the EEC where the animal survives). He quoted a rough estimate of "500 to 1,000" wolves left in Spain.

His reports and observations helped to form the basis of an action plan passed unanimously by the European parliament.

This important document pledges the full and legal protection of wolves in all the member states and urges them to implement the control of feral dogs, institute the reintroduction of natural prey, mount educational campaigns, encourage research, the protection of the habitat and the expansion of captive breeding (one "conservation" plan being mooted is the mating of wolves and German shepherd dogs for the pet market).

The long-maligned wolf was one of the first animals to be domesticated by man. But in the end, preservation efforts and charitable sentiments may not be enough to save it.

With heartfelt reluctance, Ramón Grande del Brio fears the wolf could one day be eradicated from the wild.

Conjuring up visions of these shadowy forms among the trees, he adds, "It will be much more difficult, however, to remove it from the world of imagination."

# CHAPTER FOUR

# Super Vultures

AMONG the congregation in a little Spanish church in the foothills of the Pyrenees, a group of young villagers was praying for the safety of one of this planet's rarest birds: the huge, abrasively-named lammergeyer, or bearded vulture. To them the birds are the *quebrantahuesos.*

They do more than pray for "nature's undertakers." Directed by officials of conservation organizations, this band of hardy and daring youngsters regularly drag up goat carcasses to ledges on awesome heights overlooking the lammergeyers' mountain homes. In this way these splendid soaring birds are fed.

Such feeding stations are essential to the continued existence

of this exotic species. Greyish-black, with an orange breast and impressive wings, the lammergeyer is high on the list of endangered birds. It's estimated that fewer than a hundred remain in Spain.

They have been killed by hunters in mistake for eagles, or by poison baits put down for wolves. Supplies of dead sheep and goats have dwindled with the reduction of great flocks herded by horsemen and the arrival of sophisticated methods of hygiene to keep the animals healthy.

So, as with the black and griffon vultures, the meat rejected by slaughterhouses, put out in those "vulture restaurants" in the wild, are now the chief source of food for the lammergeyer. For protection reasons, the location of these feeding stations is kept secret.

Lammergeyers, beautiful in flight but less striking on the ground, supplement the artificial feeding with a neat trick. On magnificent wings, their primaries outstretched like slim fingers, the bird will soar above rocky ground with large bones left by predators, holding the bone in its beak or in the grip of its talons. Dropping the bone from a height to crack it open on the hard terrain, the vulture lands to eat the marrow. Hence its Spanish name: "bone-breaker."

Even that basic means of nourishment is no longer available to the lammergeyer on the same scale as only 50 years ago. All Iberian-based vultures require supplies of medium to large livestock carcasses, and the lammergeyer is no exception. In the Pyrenees alone, there are no longer enough wild or stock animals to provide a regular supply of carcasses. The shy and lonely

*Previous pages: the Lammergeyer displays its awesome wingspan, at nearly three metres one of the widest in the skies.*

lammergeyer has become to a large extent dependent on the care and benevolence of man.

WITH its distinctive flight silhouette, the bird on the wing looks more like a large falcon than a carrion creature. Its wings are long and narrow-angled, the tail diamond-shaped. The eyes are ringed ruby-red. It does not have the long, bare neck many people find repulsive in vultures.

At the breeding grounds where nests are constructed with twigs and grasses in remote mountain caves on cliffs, well protected from the weather, the bird will break its normal silence with excited, high-pitched whistles. If undisturbed, lammergeyers will use the same nest, set higher than those of other vultures, year after year.

Egg-laying takes place from December until the end of February. The clutch consists of one to two — very rarely three — eggs. Most often, it consists of only one egg and when there are two the second chick rarely survives. Incubation lasts 55-58 days.

The chicks, downy little replicas of their parents, appear in late winter and early spring when the mountains are shrouded in mist or covered in snow. When rearing nestlings, the parents need considerable amounts of nourishment.

The adults are great gliders, soaring high on breezes and upward thermals, barely using their wings, as they search for the dead over scores of square miles of the landscape. In this way, the "mountain cleaners" will stay up for hours during the day. They do not fly at night, partly because their normally keen vision is restricted in the dark and partly because the thermals on which they ride the skies do not occur until the sun comes up.

The extensive home-range of the bird includes nesting sites, roosts and bone-breaking grounds.

A friend of my years in Africa, naturalist Dr Norman Myers,

*The Lammergeyer is called a "bone breaker" in Spanish, because it drops bones from a height to break them open and get at the marrow.*

sums up the role of the vulture: "He is a natural and vital component of nature's scheme, an integral part of both living and dying."

Spain's last lammergeyers are shielded by the government, but even the threat of imprisonment might not deter some eager "sportsman" from taking shots at such a fine trophy.

Experts say there is a "patchy" world distribution of lammergeyers including parts of Soviet Russia, China and African countries like Ethiopia. On the other hand, the birds are said to be extinct in such former breeding parts as mainland Italy, Switzerland, Sicily, Austria, Yugoslavia, Bulgaria and Romania.

While the last pair in the Cazorla district have now disappeared (feared poisoned with strychnine), in Spain the lammergeyer scene is not entirely dark. A record 21 chicks have been reared in one nature reserve.

It seems that while most shepherds have long regarded other large birds as enemies of the young in their flocks they have looked upon the bearded vulture with admiration and respect as a harmless but imposing "garbage man" of the mountains. And the Worldwide Fund for Nature has paid the shepherds to play their part in protecting the birds, and to leave out for them in the fields the remains of animals in their charge that die.

Such unlikely guardians and nature-lovers' feeding sites are playing their parts in efforts to ensure the lammergeyer will not remain, as one writer so vividly expressed it, "little more than a ghostly visitant from the past."

SPAIN is also one of the last homes of the equally fantastic black vulture — it's actually sooty-brown but looks jet-black from a distance — with, like the lammergeyer, a wing-span longer than the tallest man.

It is officially described by the government in Madrid as "vulnerable," with only a few hundred pairs surviving. But Spain

*Spain is home to the world's largest population of Black Vultures, but with only a few hundred pairs surviving that is not enough.*

probably boasts the world's highest population of these spectacular, carrion-eating birds.

It's scientifically named *Aegypius monachus*. Our ancestors called it "the monk of the woods," something of a misnomer for the cap on its head looks more like a cardinal's vestment. To me, the black vulture is a bewigged judge with a cold, steely stare.

Like the lammergeyer, this virtually voiceless creature belongs to desolate mountains and hills where, unlike other vultures, it builds large, accessible platforms of sticks for nests, easily looted by unscrupulous egg-collectors attracted by the birds' rarity and splendour. It has been known now and then to nest on a ledge of a cliff-face (as if to ensure protection), but generally its roost or nest is among the topmost branches of a cork- or holm-oak.

The black vulture searches daily for carrion over plains and valleys. But it too is experiencing a decrease in its food supplies as farmers change from using oxen, mules and donkeys to mechanical devices for agricultural work such as ploughing.

Today, the vultures fly long distances to find other — unnatural — supplies of food such as live rabbits. Even this has its dangers, for some have died as a result of eating diseased rabbits.

The black vulture is an accomplished glider. It "floats" in the air throughout the day. The nuptial display consists of both the male and female executing a series of geometric spirals bird people call "flying cylinders," with the aid of thermals. Following this aerial mating, as a rule only a single chick is born, from a whitish egg that has been incubated over a period of two months.

A lammergeyer is known to have lived for 40 years yet, like that breed, the black vulture needs methods — such as hatching

*The Black Vulture's nest is often large and easily accessible, making them vulnerable to unscrupulous egg hunters.*

and rearing chicks artificially '— to outstrip mortality rates with procreation. Peasants still falsely believe the black vulture preys on live lambs, and, as with other species, shooting and poisons have taken their toll over the decades.

On the credit side, there are protected breeding sites in the mountains, highlands and thickets of Avila's Sierra de Gredos, the Toledo hills, and Extremadura's Monfrague. Here, it is believed, there are well over a hundred of the species while in the Gredos region there are some 40 pairs. A long and exhaustive scientific study, valley by valley, in the Montes de Toledo in 1987 revealed 78 pairs in one of the country's largest known breeding colonies.

While there are ornithologists who fear the black vulture may disappear within the next half-century, the scales may be beginning to tip in the bird's favour.

# CHAPTER FIVE

# Antlers, Horns

# and Tusks

IT'S a paradox of nature that animals with conspicuous weapons — deer, the Spanish ibex and wild boar — are vegetarians.

Deer's antlers *can* cause death — but often it's to their owners. There's an example of this in the museum of Torre de Vinagre in the Cazorla district where two pairs of interlocked antlers are displayed. Visitors are told they belonged to contestant stags in the rutting season that died of starvation after both became helplessly trapped.

There are three kinds of the reindeer's relatives in Spain: fallow, roe and red deer. Large browsing and grazing animals, their stomachs are adapted to chewing the cud found in open

*Fallow Deer are indigenous to the Mediterranean region.*

woodland. Unless protected, they feed principally at night on grasses and acorns in glades. All deer males have antlers formed of bone, shed annually. While regrowing the antlers are covered with short-haired skin known as velvet.

Indigenous in the Mediterranean sphere, fallow deer are boldly spotted in summer, and when mating in autumn the males make rhythmic barking and grunting sounds. They fight each other with flattened, palmate antlers.

Red deer, of Scottish origin, the stags nearly the size of an elk, are the largest in Europe. Their coat is reddish-brown in summer, greyish in winter. They need trees for food and shade, and excess numbers might be culled or hunted for venison when they destroy woodlands and cause soil erosion.

Roes, with short antlers of up to three points set on a rough "coronet" ring, are among the smallest deer in Europe. Like the bigger red deer, they have a rich, reddish-brown coat in summer. Their white rump patch is faint and gives little away during those months, but it's prominent in winter.

Roe deer are usually glimpsed singly in Spanish woodlands of all kinds, near clearings or plenty of low vegetation. They form small groups in winter. After spending the day in thick cover, they emerge at twilight to feed in open ground on shrubs, broad-leaved trees and blackberry bushes.

In the rutting season in July and August, the bucks mark their territory by rubbing the bark of trees with their strong antlers until it is tattered and the trunk exposed.

Deer are killed by lynx where the cats exist, but normally only the head is eaten. This, say scientists, is neither sadism nor bloodthirstiness — "Simply," one scientist, claims, "the insolent extravagance of these proud hunters."

THE long, graceful lyre-like horns of the Spanish ibex, which dwells among rocks close to the sky, are not used to kill other animals but to threaten or, less often, to fight their peers. Generally, such clashes between these "Olympians of Goatdom" are over possession of mountain territory or for the attentions of the females. These, incidentally, have only short horns.

It's thought *Capra hispánica* originated in central Europe and was driven south into what is now Spain by the glaciers of the Ice Ages.

History books tell us the Romans watched pairs of sturdy bucks locking horns in a battle in the arenas. Unfortunately, the easiest way for them to capture an ibex to be trained to fight was to slaughter the mother and take the young.

In the Middle Ages, the animal earned a reputation for magic.

*Unafraid of humans within the protection of a Spanish natural reserve, Red Deer are the largest deer in Europe.*

Ibex blood was thought to be a cure for corns. Hair and resin taken from the big wild goat's stomach were pronounced cures for various ailments, including gout. Ruthlessly hunted to provide both medicines and food, the ibex quickly declined in numbers. They may have been interbred with domestic goats at some time, as evidenced by territorial variations of the shape of the horns.

The real danger to the Spanish ibex has never been the precarious nature of its mountain habitat, often a few steps away from a 1,500-foot drop. In modern times there have been people who almost shot the species out of existence.

"We are rather afraid the survival of these animals will only be a question of time," wrote two British naturalists after a journey through Spain in 1870. In fact, one sub-species was exterminated only a century ago.

Since then the fortunes of the ibex have waxed and waned. But it is heartening that they can once more be counted throughout the country in their tens of thousands.

They are to be found among the clouds munching alpine vegetation such as dwarf shrubs, grass, sedge and lichens. Sure-footed on the soft, rubbery soles of their hooves, they inhabit the Sierra de Gredos west of Madrid. And isolated herds are found in the mountains along the Mediterranean coast of south-east Spain — where villagers organizing illegal ibex feasts have found themselves in the hands of the Civil Guard.

At the turn of the century the ibex numbers in the Gredos mountains — today the largest population in the country — had been reduced by fashionable hunting to a dozen seemingly doomed specimens. In 1905, King Alfonso XIII ordered a six-year ban on ibex hunting, and in the following 20 years shooting the animal within the extensive royal reserve was limited to only five hunts.

By 1939, the ibex families in the Gredos had recovered to an astonishing total of 2,000 animals. And the herds continued to breed at such a rate that strictly supervised hunting, a conservation measure not often understood by the general public, was introduced in one area. In this way, over-population and consequent destruction of the feeding grounds was avoided.

Almost invisible in their greyish-brown coats as they lie in the shade of spectacular crags and escarpments, small groups of the Spanish ibex relocated from the interior live in the north's Ordesa national park among peaks towering to 11,000 feet, ideal homes for both *Capra* and the equally fleet-footed chamois.

In Andalusia there are other ibex populations. The best known to visitors occupies the Sierra de Cazorla natural park of crags 6,000 feet high, mountain meadows, waterfalls, streams and a spring which is the source of the mighty Guadalquivir river.

Contemporary breeding has been accelerated by the fact that the natural predators of the ibex — wolves, bears, lynx and eagles — have been eliminated in some mountainous regions or are themselves under threat.

But new menaces face the ibex. Get-rich-quick developers are invading the mountains with blueprints for high-rise hotels, chalet villages, ski-runs and other tourist facilities.

On the other hand, ancient beliefs persist. Peasant poachers, although principally wanting tasty meat for their cook-pots, still practise the old remedies on themselves and their families. And farmers will kill the wild ibex as a competitor for livestock grazing. Or take over a habitat for agriculture. Others cut down

*Previous pages: a classic silhouette of a Spanish Ibex, perched on an inaccessible mountain top. This page, Roe Deer, among the smallest deer in Europe.*

trees and vegetation for fuel.

There is some degree of security for the ibex, however, because it rarely deserts its lofty domain. Only in the safety of darkness will it descend below the tree-line to graze the meadows.

All extremely agile on steep rocks, females, yearlings and kids form small companies in summer. The mature males, with horns a tenth of their average body weight of 150lb., are solitary or gather in small bachelor parties of up to 50 on higher ground.

The rut takes place in winter, and kids are born in late spring or early summer. They are sure-footed almost from the time they appear. A few hours after being born, they are able to follow their mothers among the boulders in search of grasses and succulent mountain plants.

FOR hundreds of years, the simple, white *palacio* in the heart of the Coto Doñana was the hunting lodge of the dukes of Medina Sidonia. Noblemen rode out of there to hunt. Inside its walls Goya painted the Maja — reportedly the Duchess of Alba — and in the 1920s it was a holiday home for King Alfonso XIII.

Today, where they were brought to bay by Renaissance huntsmen with spears and packs of dogs, wild boar are living abundantly and peacefully within the boundaries of the national park. The *palacio* is now both a research station and guest-house for VIPs, and boar is no longer synonymous with banquets there.

Ancestors of the domestic breeds, boar are the hardiest and most widely distributed of all wild pig species.

The males have razor-sharp, nine-inch tusks to repel attackers. Those of the females are shorter and smaller, but they are still effective weapons.

Both sexes have cloven hooves, and massive heads. Yet they trot with ease and grace on twinkling feet, pushing tapering snouts along the ground as they root for acorns. They eat with

*A nature photographer has to make a hasty retreat from an uncooperative subject, a Wild Boar.*

forelegs splayed out, crunching the acorns loudly between sets of fine, sharp teeth.

Bulbs and tubers are also important to their diet. By autumn, they're fat pigs with dense, bristly coats, known to have attained weights of more than 500lb.

A mammal of the primeval dark forests that once covered Europe, the wild boar of Spain's deciduous woodlands has no enemy except man, who has persecuted it as a crop-raider and for hunting. (During both World Wars there were notable increases in wild boar populations in Europe attributed to temporary cessation of the sport.)

Ever since man developed weapons to kill at a distance, boar have developed a special wariness of him. But, unless harassed or a person gets too close to a lair of piglets, the boar is unlikely to use its tusks in assault. There have been, however, instances where both men and dogs have been gored and killed by them in old-time hunts.

*Wild Boar seldom attack, but are fiercely protective of their young.*

Nocturnal to a large degree, wary yet adaptable, the animal willingly takes to water. The males live alone or in small groups, except during the winter rutting season. During spring or early summer, the female, capable of rapidly restoring numbers, may give birth to up to 10 or 12 youngsters (and she can produce as many as three litters within a couple of years). The piglets remain in a rough nest, such as that of bent reeds, before following their mother around on foraging trips. Brown and cream stripes, which fade as they mature, provide camouflage in the brush and forests for the hungry offspring.

A wild boar was the personal emblem of King Richard III of England, and one of the country's four heraldic beasts of the chase. So it's appropriate, perhaps, that roasted haunch, saddle or shoulder of the animal has been replacing turkeys and geese as Christmas fare in some stately homes. Gourmet restaurants in Britain and other parts of Europe are increasingly adding cuts of boar, from those reared on private, free-range farms, to their menus.

The taste for boar, gamey after hanging for weeks and with a good beefy texture, declined by the end of the 18th century as a result of over-hunting, but has been revived as a profitable commercial venture. London food halls sell wild boar pâté, sausages, ham and fresh meat. There's only a limited demand, however, for that erstwhile centre-piece of royal banquets — the boar's head.

# CHAPTER SIX

# Dancing Courtships

IMAGINE a large bird sporting a Blimpish moustache of white bristles, with an ostrich-type head and legs, that barks like a dog when excited.

"A goose with eagle's wings," according to one description.

Such is the great bustard — a strange being belonging to the pages of "Alice in Wonderland" — strutting the Spanish plains and agricultural lands.

Known in Spain as the *avutarda,* this magnificent bird was once found over most of Europe. Changes in agricultural practices and burgeoning urban development have greatly restricted their range. Now they belong solely to a few open plains in Australia,

East Germany, Poland, the Balkans, the USSR, Turkey and the Iberian peninsula.

Statistics show that in Spain, as elsewhere, there has been a steady drop in the great bustard population. But the decline has been less drastic than in other parts of Europe and the Soviet Union over the years.

The Spanish picture is still grim. Between 1950 and 1960, there were an estimated 25,000 great bustards in the country. Some 22 years later that figure had slumped to a total of just over 8,000, more than half of this number being found in Castile-León. Yet, overall, Spain had more great bustards around than all the other European lands put together. (Counting is done by volunteer enumerators in cars, using grid-maps.)

Because it breeds on agricultural land, it is to the birds' advantage that much of the farming in Spain — in Andalusia, Extremadura, Castile-León and other parts — has still quite a long way to go to reach modern standards, replacing manual labour with mechanization. The bare plains have yet to be developed by mechanical monsters.

The country remains a comparative stronghold of the species, a breeding sanctuary where the nests, eggs and chicks of these ground-nesting birds — they scratch a hole in the soil in corn and other cereal fields — are, to date, less likely to be crushed by a variety of heavy machines as in other European lands. On that basis, the Iberian peninsula continues to harbour more great bustards than the total elsewhere — although in Andalusia alone, several thousands have been reduced to a couple of hundred birds in less than two decades.

One of the world's largest flying birds (weighing up to 30lb.),

*A male Great Bustard, at 30lb one of the world's largest flying birds, puts on a colourful display to attract a mate.*

they were prized game from the days of primitive man — like a turkey, it makes good eating — until recent times when they were declared fully protected in Spain.

They continue to exist in some of the earth's most vulnerable habitats, but shooters, chemical pesticides, traps and peri-urban development have cut down the birds' range and numbers. The advance of Spain's agricultural revolution, measured though it may be, will continue to pose a threat to them, for by a sad coincidence harvesting usually overlaps with the great bustard's nesting season.

Understandably shy, crouching or running swiftly at the first sign of danger, the bird walks in a slow, almost pompous, fashion on six toes with its grey head on a long, thick neck erect, wary and silent, to catch any warning.

Rising from the wheat or maize fields with a sudden "whoosh," the male bird is spectacular in flight, looking from below like a great white goose, neck outstretched and black-tipped wings beating slowly.

Some of the birds have been known to make winter visits from Spain to Africa, and proof of such trips is said to be provided by the stomach contents of dead bustards. Soldier ants and various big beetles unknown in Spain were found in one bird. Their normal diet, however, consists of cereals, frogs and local insects.

The male bird's gruff barks are heard during the springtime mating season when open spaces are essential for the breeding of the species. Without such "display grounds," the courtship ritual, one of the bird spectacles of the world, will not take place.

In the early morning when all is quiet and peaceful, there are long, communal, or single, courtship displays by the gorgeously-plumed males which, incidentally, are generally polygamous. Before the dancing rituals, elimination contests will probably be performed to establish the dominant males, or *barbons,* who will attract coteries of females.

*Disturbed by intruders, a group of Great Bustards takes to the air. The birds breed on open farmland in Spain.*

Groups of up to a hundred male birds may gather in a chosen rural arena for claw-to-claw battles, the results of which will grade their dominance in the sexual hierarchy; a literal pecking order.

Weak male youngsters eliminated as potential fathers in the contests tend to form small, pathetic bands and, rejected as non-productive specimens, will wander the terrain, not daring to approach the spots where mating is going on.

Dr K.J. Carlson, an authority on the great bustard who is among the few people to have witnessed a courtship ceremony, states:

"The males walk or trot across a huge display ground. If two males approach each other, both will suddenly stop some distance apart and begin to puff out their feathers. The wings droop to the ground so that the white feathers are turned 'inside-out.' The tail is spread and raised over the back to reveal more white feathers. The head and neck are thrown back, glandular pouches on either side of the neck are inflated, and moustachial bristles in front of their eyes stand straight up."

Dr Carlson and his party watched a pair of great bustards actually mating.

"The male circled round the female, beating her with his left wing until she was flattened to the ground; he then mounted her before an audience of several females."

Each male may mate with up to five females, which are always in the majority.

After fertilization, a female will go off to find an area of cereals or long grass in which to make her nest. She incubates two or three olive green and brown blotched eggs over a period of 21 to28 days. Hatchlings may be preyed upon by ravens, their chief enemy, but the young leave the nest soon after hatching, and for a few days are fed plant shoots by their mother.

When there's any sign of danger each family group will fly off in close formation as a security measure. Inexpert youngsters may land far from their mothers, who will rush to collect them in response to their mewing cries of distress.

While the females are busy rearing and training their young, the *barbons* congregate in groups. During the winter, they form larger groups with the females and juveniles. In early spring, the birds disperse, returning to their breeding grounds.

THERE was excitement in England recently, aroused by stories in the national press that five great bustards, driven from eastern Europe by intense cold, had been seen for a while in the fields of Suffolk.

The birds used to nest in Britain but became extinct there in the 19th century, the last recorded nest being on Salisbury plain in 1830. Evidence of its plight in Victorian days is contained in a serio-comic anecdote concerning an aristocratic shooting party.

Among the guests of the host, Lord Pembroke, was a foreign ambassador known to be an erratic shot. So he was told that, while the rest of the party killed pheasants, he would be sent off across Salisbury plain with a keeper for a rare and privileged treat: a great bustard shoot.

In the late afternoon Lord Pembroke and his fellow guns returned to the manor house feeling guilty at having deceived the ambassador. Sure enough, they found him in a filthy temper.

"I have indeed had a poor day," he told his host. "I walked and walked and walked, but only managed to shoot three of those damned big birds."

In the winters of the Fifties, there were great congregations of bustards on the Spanish lowlands. Today they gather in far lesser numbers.

With shooting reduced to a minimum, the creation of special grassland "reserves" and the introduction of captive breeding of specimens are among the methods suggested by experts to stabilize and increase the great bustard's numbers. Biologists are assisting by monitoring the species' life patterns with plastic leg-tags.

And it is encouraging to record that the birds themselves are co-operating with nature in resisting the threats that confront them: females once took three to four years to reach sexual maturity, the males about five years. Now, many great bustard hens are ready for mating at the age of two years, and the males at between two and three years.

# CHAPTER SEVEN

# Rara Avis

A PART from the great bustard, there are one or two other Spanish birds international ornithologists delight in seeing and studying.

One of them is the *urogallo*, also known as the capercaillie, a giant grouse whose rich plumage, amorous pursuits and mating ceremonies rival those of the bustard.

But its long and measured sexual rituals, performed in the highlands of the north, can be fatal. The efforts of courtship dull the *urogallo's* senses of self-defence. And it can become a gargantuan meal for birds of prey, like the fearsome eagle owl *(Bubo bubo)* which strikes at dawn when the display has begun.

The male *urogallo*, with its glossy black-brown plumage, a

blue-green chest, and scarlet skin-patches above the eyes, is proudly independent. Again like the great bustard, it is polygamous and boasts a harem of hens. His mating display is a colourful show. He stands on a rock before a group of comparatively unglamorous females with his beautiful tail fanned out like that of a peacock. At the same time, his ivory-white beak is raised — for minutes, for hours — in wild, guttural love-calling.

In general, the cock calls to his females and fellow males with a quiet song, beginning with "tik-up, tik-up," which accelerates rapidly. And ends with a "pop" like a cork being drawn from a wine bottle. This may be followed by a short phase of grating, whispered notes.

Except in winter, when the ground may be rock-hard or covered in snow, the hens rarely fly up into the trees. They are of a comparatively unimpressive earth-brown colour which normally serves to hide them on the ground.

In snowy conditions, the females inhabit the more open parts of the woods where the wind is likely to disperse the snow fall. In temperate weather they keep to the warmest spots among the trees where there are insects to ensure the nourishment of their chicks. The male is literally shady, staying among the shadows most of the day.

If obliged to take to the air, the *urogallo's* flight is brief, with alternate spells of rapid wing-beats and long glides. Hens nest among the undergrowth at the foot of a pine tree, or in protective scrub on open high ground. The lordly cock-bird takes no part in the domestic duties of any of its wives. The birds all feed on berries, shoots, buds and certain kinds of insects.

*The open-air nuptial display of the Capercaillie makes this increasingly rare bird vulnerable to its enemies.*

There may well be a couple of thousand *urogallos* in Spain at the present time but their numbers are endangered through reafforestation for the lumber industries, hunting (although the bird is protected by the provisions of the Berne Convention), mountain safaris for visitors in overland vehicles, and developments for winter sports in the Pyrenees.

Aiming to find ways of increasing the birds' protection, young Spanish ecologists are briefly capturing male *urogallos* and fitting one of their legs with a tiny radio transmitter before releasing them, to monitor their activities and habits. So far, it has been established the otherwise elusive *urogallo* males have special, chosen places in the wild where they put on those displays to win over the hens. At times there are several cock-birds on show, challenging each other for the attention of the females.

Sometimes there's a struggle, conducted even more fiercely when one male does not accept the superiority of the other. The contestants use their beaks to jab and wound each other but, by some inbred rule of nature, never employ their claws. The fight is closely followed by hens, who watch in silence from the grandstand of low branches of a tree. The victor is assured of a warm welcome.

The riotous scene, enacted in bleeps and burps over the earphones of researchers concealed long distances away, goes on over two months of every year. Reproduction follows.

ON noisy wings, their necks and legs outstretched, hundreds of greater flamingos, a striking combination of crimson, pink and black, flew low above my head in serried ranks.

It was twilight, making the scene at Fuente de Piedra lagoon north of Málaga magical. The sky was transformed into an aerial rose garden.

One of Europe's ornithological treasures, the greater flamingo, in flight or wading, is among the most attractive, and at the same time bizarre, creations of nature. Its slow, measured steps on stilt-like legs contrast dramatically with the wild Andalusian "tap dance" which in Spanish has the same name as the bird.

The big stretch of Fuente de Piedra water is one of the flamingos' principal feeding grounds in Spain. They are also to be found in colonies in salt marshes, shallow coastal lakes, flood-waters and mud-flat estuaries like Doñana in southern parts of the country.

My friend and colleague John Reader — photographer, author and naturalist — who has made a close study of the bird writes:

"Its legs allow it to wade sedately and feed in water up to three feet deep. Frequently algae-rich waters are shallower than this so a long neck is essential for reaching the surface. If the flamingo were to keep its head upright when feeding, it would need an extra kink in the neck. It solves the problem by feeding with its head upside down."

The birds harvest nutritious algae by "grazing" on the top inch or so of water.

The interior of their bills is equipped with an amazing filtering mechanism, consisting of rows of fine, hairy growths, about a hundred to the inch. Water is sucked in and out trapping the algae on which the flamingo feeds.

This system of sustenance has all the precision of a delicate scientific process.

Reader adds: "When feeding, a flamingo submerges its bill in the water — upside down — and a rapid pulse of water can be seen booming out of the beak.

"The lower mandible, which is uppermost in the feeding position, is cellular and filled with air spaces. It is so light it will float like a cork if detached from the bird's head. This buoyancy allows flamingos to feed in choppy water without continually having to use energy in adjusting the height of their heads to

compensate for waves."

Strictly gregarious, the greater flamingos "talk" to their companions with many trumpeting cries of "ar-honk" and, particularly when flying in formation, a goose-like gabble. They breed colonially, building circular mud-heap nests a few inches above the brackish water in shallows where virtually no other birds breed.

By April, each pair of flamingos has usually produced a single egg. This is hatched after about a month, among an assembly of mud-pie nests.

A forest of adult red legs will conceal most of the dark plumage of the greyish-brown young who are weak, puny and vulnerable in comparison with their lordly parents. The chicks are "a floating carpet" as they struggle to keep up with their slowly-moving elders on the feed.

The greater flamingos favour the subtropical climate of southern Spain where a plentiful supply of algae, molluscs and crustaceans has been assured. But a good food supply and a benign climate are not enough.

The high total of greater flamingos in Spain — some unofficial estimates have numbered them in thousands — is deceptive. Swollen figures tossed around without benefit of scientific census hide the fact that the population has been decreasing in recent years.

Several factors contribute to this tragic situation in which disastrous breeding seasons have dramatically reduced the numbers of flamingo chicks.

Diversion of water for irrigation schemes has depleted lagoons

*Previous pages: Greater Flamingos congregate in shallow lagoons in southern Spain to breed. Right, a flamingo strikes a typical pose as it wades through the water in search of microscopic food.*

and other water habitats, and operations are under way to pipe much more water from inland regions to coastal resorts. Prolonged drought in searing "greenhouse" summers is another danger, shrinking or drying up the water completely and destroying the food it contains. Lakes become salt-pans, and the story-book birds can only breed successfully in certain years.

Some of the birds end up snared and choked on barbed wire fences around agricultural and other land. And hunters take their toll of these slow, graceful flyers. They make absurdly easy targets — sorely evidenced by the fact that in a single weekend near Algeciras not so long ago 200 of them were shot.

It's hard to see why anyone should want a stuffed flamingo in his parlour.

# CHAPTER EIGHT

# Voices in the Night

T HE setting in western Spain was idyllic. A weathered
*granja* with its own water-wheel on a clear stream,
surrounded by flowering shrubs. Olive trees marched
up the hillside.

And in the pale light of a crescent moon all was serene. Then
the small hours of the morning were shattered by a cacophony of
what sounded to me like the rapid clucking and clicking of a
hundred hens. This went on for an hour or so.

At breakfast, our English companions' nine-year-old son
Jonathan wanted to know: "What were all those funny voices in
the night?"

Our host chuckled. "The farm-workers say they're midwife

toads. But in the six years I've been here I've never seen one," he said.

He's unlikely to do so. Over the years, biologists were frustrated in their searches for this sensitive, shy and delicate creature, and had to abandon attempts to record its strange voice. Never more than two inches long, *Alytes cisternasii* is yet another natural rarity indigenous to Spain.

The bug-eyed, short-legged Spanish midwife toad is one of the thousands of species of tailless amphibians. Yet it is found only in the Iberian peninsula. Mottled brown, small and chubby, it frequents the reedy banks of rivers and digs lone burrows in the sand or soft earth with its clawed forelegs.

It is secretive to the point where it stays underground and becomes a daytime hermit. It rarely emerges from its burrow except under the cover of night. And then only to breed or to feed on insects, earthworms, spiders and snails.

A unique mating process — prosaically recorded in scientific parlance as "a highly specialized reproduction adaptation" — gives this game little toad its name.

Unlike related species, the midwife toad mates on land and not in the water. But there have been very few scientific observations of the ritual in its habitat. As part of their personal security system and highly reclusive nature, both governed by their size, the Spanish midwife toads will stop their puffed-up, croaking calls to each other if there is any movement or bright light near them. They are, therefore, particularly difficult to photograph, or observe, in their environment.

In 1741, a French scientist named Demours was among the first

*A model father: the Midwife Toad with a cargo of eggs. Extremely shy, the Midwife Toad is difficult to observe in its environment.*

to draw attention to the existence of the gross and ungainly midwife toad and its fascinating form of reproducing its kind. According to a later, four-year study, after nocturnal mating calls have been repeated for some time (at 60 or more a minute) the roaming males and females make themselves known to each other. And the performance begins.

It seems that the mounted male toad clasps the chosen female round the waist with his forelegs and keeps her in his grasp — sometimes for hours — until she spawns a mass of minute, yellowish eggs which are then fertilized by the male. The eggs are attached to long, strong strings of jelly and, dipping into the glutinous egg-mass with one leg and then another, the male adroitly wraps the tiny "beads" round his hind legs. The egg-thread is used to bind them and keep them in place.

The partners separate 10 to 20 minutes after the male has taken on his burden. He retires to a warm and humid hiding place with his glistening load and will wait for anything from three weeks to over a month before he receives a biological "nod" that the larvae are ready to hatch. One moonless night he struggles down to the water from his hideout, jumps in and immerses the eggs in a pool, or the river itself if it is not flowing too swiftly.

The eggs hatch within two hours (enzymes in the sacs release the embryos) to become free-swimming tadpoles. As the last one appears, the amphibian midwife scrapes off the empty egg envelopes and returns to the land for a period of rest in his burrow.

Before long, however, he'll resume his mating calls to invite carrying another batch of eggs.

A resolute and dedicated worker in the cause of his species, it's believed to be routine for him to carry eggs for hatching three times in a single year.

A close relative of the Spanish toad is *Alytes obstetricans* which is distinguished at close quarters by having *three* tubercules on the palm of its hand while the Iberian variety has only two.

Toads that mate in water develop in-season swellings on palms and fingers from which small spines protrude. These, known as "nuptial pads," are used to get a firm grip on the female's slippery body in the pool or stream. Mating on land, where the partner's skin is abrasive and dry, the midwife-toad does not have, nor does it need, these "nuptial pads."

Early this century, studies of *Alytes obstetricans* were made by a distinguished Austrian academic, Dr Paul Kammerer, whose work was linked to the origins of man. It aroused an international scientific war, and became the basis of a major Russian film and a book, "The Case of The Midwife Toad" by Arthur Koestler, deeply concerned with evolutionary theories.

Dr Kammerer was virtually alone in his ability to capture and rear midwife toads. Techniques of breeding this toad required patience and close attention over many years and several generations of the species.

Modern zoologists' experiments have been limited by the fact that it is difficult to breed the midwife toad unless, as Dr Kammerer pointed out, the researcher is willing and prepared to devote a large part of his or her life to the work. He was one of the few who did so.

The toad keeps a low profile of ugliness and most mammalian carnivores avoid it. They are scared of poison in its warty skin thanks to which humans have associated it with witches, the macabre and evil. Snakes and carrion crows are their principal enemies. But first these have to find their toad.

From 1558, any stone, some precious, likened to a toad in shape and colour, or supposed to have been formed in the body of a toad, was worn as a jewel, set in a ring or as a lucky charm and protection against evil.

The most coveted and valued kind of stone was one fabled to have been found in the head of a toad.

The toads' reputation for being deadly poisonous appears to have started in 1629. Attendants of charlatans at court went through the motions of eating toads to enable their masters to claim their skills in overcoming a lethal meal — a sort of royal sideshow. The word "toady" — to attend to with servility from interested motives" — may have arisen from these ghoulish tricks. Or perhaps as a result of the activities of that cold-blooded but model father, the midwife toad.

CHAPTER NINE

# Black Stork, Red Fox

R ESTING in the shade of a cork-oak in Extremadura one spring afternoon, I heard above me the sound of a saw cutting wood.

It seemed a strange place for carpentry. Peering through the foliage I saw a big, exotic bird with black plumage perched on a large, untidy nest. It was uttering hoarse, gasping noises, like that of a saw being used, but leavened the performance with musical notes.

Accomplishing a hazardous and hungry trans-desert marathon, the black stork was back in Spain after its winter sojourn in Africa, back to the nest it had used the previous year.

Unlike the larger, more numerous, adaptable and extrovert

white variety of the species which nests on tall chimneys, church towers and other high structures, the shy black stork prefers rocky platforms high in the mountains, or oak and elm trees. These, unfortunately, are as threatened as the birds themselves — by mushrooming urbanisation and the pumping of ground water into the systems of cities and towns.

Loss of traditional nesting spots all over Spain in the onset of modernization has already drastically reduced the numbers of black storks. And their habitats are now confined to a few areas in the west of the country. The current population of *cigüeña negra* in Spain is said to be numbered in mere hundreds. In 1987, in what was claimed to be the first-ever black stork census in the country, it was estimated only 175 couples were living in Spain.

The destruction of their breeding places began in the Sixties with the cutting down of Mediterranean forests and the poisoning with industrial chemicals of watering places like streams and lakes where the bird went for food such as frogs. Some, or course, were shot as "souvenirs," others have died on high-tension cables.

A stork in most respects except for its deeply dark feathers (and it does have a white chest), the *cigüeña negra* frequents rivers, lagoons or marshes surrounded by woods. A solitary bird in some respects, it flies singly or in small parties during the southern migration and back, over the Straits of Gibraltar. Averse to moving their heavy wings continually, storks fly by gliding and need thermal up-currents to maintain altitude. Since there are practically no thermals over large expanses of water, the birds do not normally fly the broadest stretches of the sea but concentrate on the shortest possible crossing for the overwater journey.

*Previous pages: unlike its white cousin, which will nest on buildings, the Black Stork nests on trees that are as threatened as the bird itself.*

On arrival from Africa, they search for places to build their nests, deep in old forests or other locations not frequented by man. Others seek out their old nests. New nests are made with twigs lined with grass, roots and moss to make a comfortable bed for the chicks. The nests are camouflaged or hidden as much as possible.

The black stork shares a curious habit with its white counterpart. On emerging from the egg, the hatchling lays its head on its back and makes rapid snapping movements with its bill to signal it's hungry. This is the preliminary stage in the bird's lifetime of characteristic clacking of its red bill, the stork's "language."

At first there is no sound because the young stork's bill is soft. But after a few weeks slight noises can be heard as the youngsters make it clear that it's time to feed them with beetles, fieldmice and grasshoppers.

The habit stays with them, getting louder and more prolonged. Basically, it can signal love or excitement — although on the ground it looks like a bad-humoured intention to attack.

Male and female black storks look alike but they behave differently. The male's courtship — preening his wings, leaping into the air and seizing nest-sticks — signals his sex and intentions to other storks. The demonstration attracts a mate who must make the correct female response. Together, the pair, heads thrown back, engage in a riot of mutual bill-clapping followed by wearied wing-flapping.

The laying of the eggs, three to five of white with a light greenish sheen, occurs a couple of days after the mating. Male and female share the responsibility for hatching, averaging 35 to 40 days. The birds rotate the eggs during this period to obtain an evenness of body heat.

The chicks emerge from the eggs with soft, snowy-white feathers, an orange beak and greenish-grey legs. For at least three

weeks from this time, the adults never leave the young on their own. When one of the parents goes off to search for food, the other remains to guard the nest.

As parents, the storks are exceptionally faithful. The male, for instance, will remain alone and sit on the eggs or rear the chicks should his partner be killed or die.

If all goes well, from the outset the parents will teach the youngsters defences against such intruders as the wild cat, lynx or eagle owl. By midsummer they are ready to leave the nest, and require virtually no tuition from their parents on how to fly.

Not sexually mature until the age of four, the young may stay in Africa in their early years. Others, drawn by some powerful, in-born call, will fly back to where they believe the nest in which they came to life in Spain still stands. Too often, they search in vain.

WHY do brown bears have no tails? Legend has it that in Europe long ago the cunning red fox persuaded a bear to try to catch fish by putting its tail through a hole in the ice of a mountain pool... With the bear's tail in it, the hole froze solid and the fox was able to attack and kill the helpless animal!

An unlikely story; even a trapped bear is capable of inflicting a great deal of damage on an enemy; and he would make an impossibly large meal for foxes, who feed on rodents, small birds and their eggs, rabbits and garbage. Some surplus food is buried, and during autumn the foxes vary their diet with fruit and berries.

When his hair was down to his waist and he wore a jacket of deerskin, Marcos, the feral boy of the Sierra Morena, numbered

*Sly and adaptable, the Red Fox thrives from the coldest mountain tops to the hottest plains of Spain.*

a vixen among his wild animal companions.

"One day when I was opening up a rabbit, a fox came up to me. I gave her a piece and she ate it, as calm as anything. Later she came back to where I was... When I was bigger, thirteen or fourteen or fifteen years old, I was king of the valley. The fox would come with me. I called her 'dog' because I thought she was a dog."

Like the wolf, the red fox (*zorro* in Spanish) is a member of the dog family, and has a high-pitched bark. It is easily distinguished by its narrow muzzle, large erect ears and long bushy tail, usually with a white tip. The coat is a rich reddish-brown. In Spain, their habitat is mainly woodland, but they can also be found on open moorland, highlands, farmland and even the perimeters of residential areas. By day, they may be seen under bushes where they are undisturbed or in short burrows of earth they have dug themselves.

Versatile and harassed, the red fox has to feed at night on small prey. Its renowned craftiness has enabled it to adapt, better than other carnivores, to man-made changes in the environment.

Although five is the usual number, there may be up to 10 cubs in a den. All of which can consume enormous quantities of rats or voles. Encouraged to breed on one hand so that it can be hunted, the fox on the other has been persistently persecuted for its depredations on poultry.

Over the centuries, the lore on foxes has accumulated. The real truth about their private lives has only recently been revealed thanks to radio tracking and other technical aids. At one time the fox was held to be one of the few monogamous mammals. The dog fox was seen to remain with the vixen and brought food to the cubs while she was rearing them. On the other score, dog foxes had a reputation of being lone nomads.

Modern research has revealed a variable social system. Some foxes *are* solitary, wandering over long distances, but the majority

*A hunter proudly displays his fox pelts. In many parts of Spain, the fox is classified as vermin and fetches a bounty.*

live together in fairly large territories. The "owners" of such areas, it's recorded, range from a single pair of foxes to a group of half a dozen adults and their offspring. A group usually consists of one male and several vixens, probably related.

Cubs, a delightful bundle of eyes and noses, are born in the spring, usually in an underground burrow. Usually only the dominant vixen gives birth. The others act as "nursemaids," guarding the young and later bringing them food.

For the first three weeks of their lives the cubs keep warm by huddling with their mother. Then she spends her days resting from their attentions and lets the "nursemaids" take over.

At the age of six weeks, a fortnight after they have started taking solid food, the cubs are taught the art of catching prey for themselves on a series of hunting trips led by their mother.

Foxes are intelligent, opportunistic hunters whose diet might range from a pheasant to blackberries and caterpillars. Lamb-stealing is likely to be the work of a single adult fox who has developed a taste for livestock.

The fur trade remains a serious threat to the species. A steep rise in prices for fashionable pelts would stimulate a demand that exceeded the birthrate and lead to a drastic decline in the numbers of the animal. Silver foxes, farmed for their furs, are a variety of the red fox but do not occur in the wild in Europe.

The fox in general is still distributed around the globe. They can live either in the icy arctic, in the torrid desert of Australia (where they were introduced at the end of the last century by a hunting club) or even in urban areas of Britain, in each case easily adapting themselves to environmental changes. In dire straits, they will risk their lives by raiding rubbish bins in towns.

Spanish studies show that, like the wolf, fox territories, well-defined and used throughout their lives, are circular in shape, for defence purposes. In search of food, the fox always uses the same paths — treating its imprints with a glandular fluid easy to recognize in the dark. Such precautions are important. Should an orphan cub or a young female in heat wander off, they are in danger of being attacked and killed by a lynx — where those are still to be found.

*Zorro,* of necessity, possesses a self-regulated reproduction mechanism. If there are no threats to existence, the birthrate of cubs remains normal. When the foxes are menaced and mortality is high, the vixen instinctively increases the number of young she bears, making her own vital contribution to the survival of her kind.

# CHAPTER TEN

# African Mysteries

W ITH arid, sun-scorched desertlands, and pock-marked lunar terrain, much of southern Andalusia is the Sahara of Spain.

Here dwell two creatures — a mammal and a reptile — that rightly belong to Africa just over the water: the curiously named ichneumon of the weasel and mongoose clans, and Europe's only tree-dwelling chameleon.

As proof of its African origins, the normal diet of the ichneumon is crocodiles' eggs. The animal is equipped with swift reflexes which make all the difference between life and death when snatching an egg within reach of snapping reptilian jaws. Or tackling a cobra. In Spain the snakes on which it preys for food do not have deadly fangs, and in Doñana they enjoy an unlimited supply of water-birds' eggs.

About the same build as polecats and mink, gluttons who will take protein wherever they can find it, the ichneumon will even catch and kill fully-grown wild ducks which abound in Doñana. They will seize animals smaller than themselves, and eat large ones if they are dead. They are great scavengers, exploratory and inquisitive. They poke into every niche and cranny, ever ready to make a change of fare with whatever they find there, be it rabbits, rodents or reptiles. Where harassed, the ichneumon is mainly nocturnal, but more active by day than most carnivores of its size, especially at dawn. Distinguished by a long body with a rather coarse and grizzled coat, short legs and ears, and a long, tapering tail, it is strictly terrestrial — even in what were, way back, foreign grounds.

It uses rocky hillsides as look-out posts for prey, standing erect on its hind feet. They are lone hunters, the exceptions being the young — usually two to four in a litter — who remain with their mother for several months while being trained in fieldcraft.

As one would imagine, the ichneumon is adept at breaking eggs to swallow the contents. Using the same method as their relatives in Africa, they nimbly toss the egg backward, between their legs, against a rock.

Slender and wiry enough to squeeze into the birds' burrows, the ichneumon now and then raids colonies of bee-eaters, seizing the chicks or eggs.

The animal has — in striking miniature — a somewhat prehistoric look. It can climb trees, though it is no expert, tightly gripping the trunk with its claws and scrambling down again, tail first. The ichneumon deposits an anal scent on tree trunks, the ground or rocks to define the area of its family territory.

They make engaging, nimble and mischievous pets — as Roman women who liked to own and display exotic creatures

*Little is known about the Ichneumon, a relative of the mongoose that has made its home in Spain.*

found. They are sometimes kept in country homes to guard against vipers.

At one time, the population was widespread in Spain. But the species is now virtually restricted to the south-west of the country, although some have been captured in the past in Leon.

Although the ichneumon has been around for a very long time, it's one of the least-known carnivores of the Iberian peninsular, as far as its general life-style in the wilderness is concerned. Relatively little is yet on scientific record in Spain regarding the nitty-gritty of its biology and ecology.

To provide a clearer picture, Dr Miguel Delibes, best known for his lynx research, has inaugurated in Doñana the sustained radio tracking of a quartet of ichneumons. Through the monitoring of these animals and visual observations, field-workers keep daily records of where, what and when the animals hunt and eat; the nature of courtships, breeding routines, and gestation periods; what ground is covered in this hairy oddity's wanderings, nocturnal or otherwise; defence tactics, and so on.

The image of this particular "African" animal is now becoming much more sharply defined.

I T hardly seems likely the chameleon walked to southern Spain when the two land masses were joined. At the strange reptile's funereal pace, the journey would have taken countless life-spans.

Yet the Spanish inhabitant is undoubtedly a member of a large African family, wonderfully adapted, with a prehensile tail and clawed toes, to grasping branches and twigs when stealthily advancing on insect meals.

In this age they are reminders that even harmless and grotesque small creatures are under threat — for they live in coastal areas favoured by real estate companies for holiday developments. And farmers want the land for hardy crops like maize.

On the other hand, it's comforting to know that if their usual habitats are taken over and destroyed, chameleons can be raised domestically from captured males and females, and the young introduced to a comparatively safe part of the wilderness.

Chameleons are some of the most intriguing creations of nature and have a special place in the zoological world. Both sexes have prominent, unwieldy-looking heads in which the movements of protruding, ball-in-socket eyes are weirdly independent.

Photographer John Reader, who bred a colony of chameleons (and I was able to follow some of its progress), writes:

"The turreted eyes swivel about, taking in colour and looking for prey in an almost total sphere of vision. When one eye sights a prey item, the other sweeps parellel to fix the object in a binocular stare. Prey suitability, distance and angle are judged in an instant."

The chameleon's slender and sticky tongue — sometimes its own length — prepares to come into play.

"The chameleon's tongue clearly takes the insect completely by surprise. The alternate tactic for the chameleon would be to rush and snap. But insects (like flies) are fast and have good eyesight. A hungry beast the size of a chameleon would have a small chance of sneaking up on its prey. So the chameleon forsakes speed of movement.

"It moves slowly along branches with a quaint rocking motion that has the rhythm of a leaf swaying in the wind. As it moves, special pigment cells just under the skin expand and contract to produce effects which imitate the colours the eyes see and the brain interprets.

"A small bone flicks the tongue clear of the jaws, and with a hydraulic surge it inflates forward like a child's party favour.

"Pressure is released, the tongue snaps back and the meal is quickly finished."

For such an amazing, camouflaged kill, the chameleon might hang far out from one limb of a tree over another, rather like a circus acrobat. Its anchoring tail and rear claws clutch the branch from which it operates.

From this far-out stance, the chameleon strikes. The sticky end of its tongue, the reptile's fundamental food weapon, is aimed at the head of the unwary insect — to kill or, possibly, to stun it.

The reptile hunts in the daytime, searching only by the sight of those swivelling eyes. After a victim is located at rest or flying in the immediate vicinity, the chameleon approaches with deadly slowness, until in range of a grasshopper, fly or some other form of insect, winged or otherwise.

It calculates the range to a fraction of an inch. Once in

position, the tongue shoots out at the speed of a lightning flash. The victim has no chance of escape from this marksman. Caught on the withdrawn tongue, the insect is eaten on the spot with the aid of the chameleon's two front claws. It has strong jaws to masticate its victims.

It's a greedy predator. Researchers have seen a lone specimen catch and devour scores of insects within a few hours.

The chameleon's principal and popular claim to biological fame is, of course, its ability to change colour. It's true that in many instances — but not every one — it can do so to adapt to its surroundings when hunting and to remain hard to spot by its prey. Changes of body colour, however, are also due to temperatures, light and, as demonstrated by the scientist Ramón y Cajal in 1902, physical factors such as sexual attraction, combativity and sickness. It seems that when dying the reptile will assume the same colouration as it does when asleep. Except during mating, the females are generally greenish in colour, the males light brown to greyish.

The periods of mating and reproduction, beginning at the end of June and going on until October, lead to a variety of colours being displayed by both sides. The males show off a livery of yellow and green spots which become more intense in the presence of a female. She becomes dusty-green with decorative flecks of white.

For copulation, usually lasting three to seven minutes, the male steals up behind the female and laboriously mounts her. She's held forcibly in the grip of his claws while they mate.

In the fervour of copulation, the female acquires colours ranging from yellow-green to plain yellow and white. During

*Previous pages: the striking Chameleon, equipped with independently swivelling eyes that enable it to scan the shrubbery in search of insects.*

pregnancy, establishing her own territory and snapping at any intruders to ward them off, she takes on a greyish hue, hard to detect against the chosen background.

The female bears 10 to 30 little white eggs, according to her size. Laying time is in autumn, generally the second fortnight of October.

The tiny, newly-hatched youngsters soon face up to life. Even before completely dry, they are independent. They will flick their tongues at the first insect they ever see, and are able to change colour like their parents. The growth of the youngsters is rapid — although they are not immediately sexually mature — and they double in size by the end of a year.

## CHAPTER ELEVEN

# Bears on the Brink

EVERYONE — well, almost everyone — loves a bear, or at least finds it fascinating. They stand like a human being, epitomize great strength, and the cubs are winsome and eminently cuddly. The bear features in the stellar constellation, heraldic devices and primitive rock paintings which show that worship of the shaggy giants was once common in Europe.

Up to the end of the last century a thousand Spanish brown bears roamed the woodlands of the Cordillera Cantábrica, the impressive mountain range in the north which embraces Asturias to the west and Leon, Palencia and Cantabria in the east.

Little more than half a century ago the bears were ruthlessly

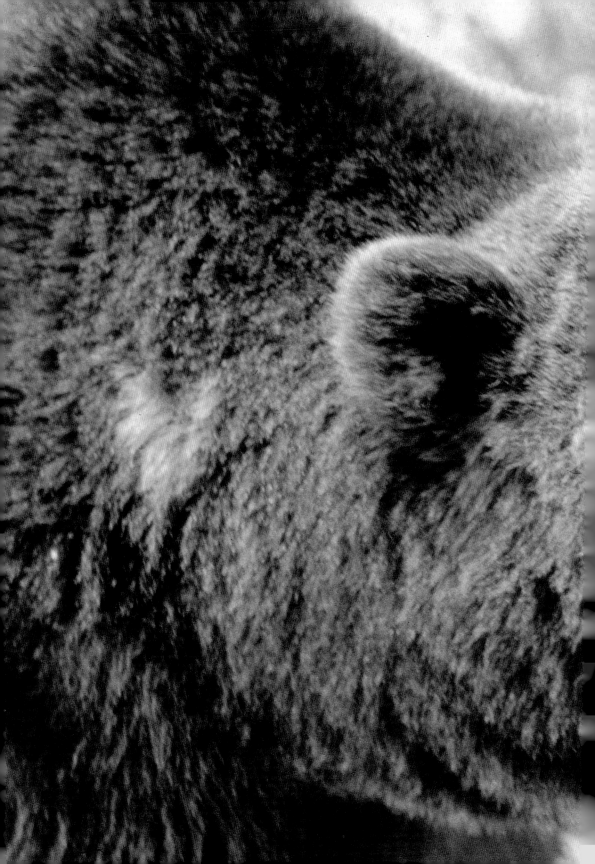

pursued among the crags for sport by aristocratic hunters on horseback and, as a result of a number of other factors, the entire bear population has shrunk to around 80 males, females and youngsters.

Although the bears have been legally protected since 1973 (and hunting and killing is banned by a royal decree carrying fines of millions of pesetas and, possibly, a year in prison) there are still people who want a bear rug by the fire or a snarling head on the wall.

Writing in the magazine *BBC Wildlife,* Teresa Farino, an authority on biographical zones and their wildlife, who divides her time between Britain and Spain's Picos de Europa, believes international poaching rings may be supplying such trophies, or guiding foreign hunters to the source. It is acknowledged that wealthy collectors are to blame for some of the worst depredations which have brought the Spanish brown bears to their present pitiful numbers.

There are other considerations. Current statistics show that in less than a decade 25 bears were poisoned by strychnine (accidentally or otherwise). Nine, including a female with her cub, were killed in Asturias alone, and the skin of a fine, 200-kilo specimen slaughtered in Leon province was smuggled out of the country and sold for £15,000.

While there's not a single case on record of one of Spain's bears attacking a person without cause (with an inbred fear of humans they will only do so if wounded or are defending their young), a man who shot dead a large male during a deer shoot in Palencia, claimed he fired in self-defence.

*Previous page: a Brown Bear can be aggressive during the rutting season, but they generally avoid humans and few attacks on man have been reported.*

The victim, with wounds in the back, was subsequently beheaded by a jubilant crowd.

BEAR paws appear on the menu in some Hong Kong restaurants. They are, like powdered rhino horn, expensive and falsely considered to be an aphrodisiac. So is another "delicacy" — ground bear's gall-bladder, sold in some parts of Asia for as much as £400 a pinch. In Macao even soup made from these ingredients is thought to be a powerful pick-me-up.

These myths are, of course, related to the size and power of the creatures.

The bears of the Cordillera Cantábrica, a sub-species of *Ursus arctos* and a smaller cousin of the American grizzly, have had to suffer appalling fates over the years.

In comparatively recent times the brown bears have been driven out of the northern foothills and scattered as a result of strip mining, road and rail tourist development, lawless hunters and timber industries, and forced to take refuge high among the snowy peaks of the entire mountain range. The hotly opposed creation of a vast reservoir at Riaño in the León uplands has threatened the existence of a sub-population of the bears.

And shepherds have accused bears of taking sheep and lambs, though prolonged studies have shown that merely 12 to 15 per cent of the animals' diet is composed of meat. Only a small proportion of that is likely to be mutton.

Continued disturbance by a variety of human activities has made all the Spanish bears extremely shy and wary. Remaining most of the time in wooded areas, they have become semi-nocturnal.

Even experts who study the Bruins rarely see one. They have to rely mainly on scratch marks, droppings, paw-prints and so on to monitor the animals' activities and habits.

At one time it seemed certain that, like their erstwhile kin in Britain, the Spanish bears were doomed to vanish entirely. Yet families continue to survive — just — in those secluded alpine forests of oak and beech.

The seven-foot-tall brown bear, one of the earth's largest land animals, has an excellent sense of smell, and its hearing is so acute it is said to be able to hear the clicking of a rifle bolt on the other side of a valley. Although they appear to be lumbering beasts, they can achieve dashes of up to 30mph, enough to bring down a roe fawn or a chamois kid which they kill swiftly by a powerful twist of the prey's neck.

Bears are often loners with a "gypsy" streak. Normally evasive, an adult male, or boar, weighing over 500 lb. might roam miles from one location to another, covering, perhaps, three times as much territory as the females whom they pursue during the early summer breeding. season.

The massive males, ears torn or misshapen, battle scars showing through their coppery fur, are roaring, ill-tempered creatures during the periods of procreation. It is a savage wooing, and rivals are fought off on all fours — for bears do not usually attack in a standing stance, as generally believed.

Females may be ready for breeding at the age of three years, and the lifetime of the average bear ranges from 15 to 34 years.

The home territories of different bears may overlap, but the larger the bear, whether a despotic male or an over-protective female, the wider the berth its fellows may give it.

In the winter den, usually a cave, a rock crevice or even a hollow tree, the sow lies, after giving birth, with her head behind

*Brown Bears have been forced to take refuge in the remoter corners of Spain's Cordillera Cantábrica.*

her hind paws, making a warm circle around her blind, furless cubs. She will have a litter of one to four. Now and then, a cub will utter a muted cry for milk like a human baby, splay its claws, or give a sleepy feline hiss.

On their bed of leaves during hibernation — actually a long, light sleep — the respiration of the boar and his mate will go down to about five breaths every couple of minutes, and their heartbeats become accordingly slow. Yet the bears' temperatures drop only 10 per cent. Once or twice a day, the animals' pulses quicken, and they come out of their slumber into almost sudden consciousness. They lie there awake in the den for a while, then drift off to sleep again.

The bears eat little or nothing for nearly half a year; but at the end of the long winter months the adults still have two-thirds of their fat to live on in the spare months of spring.

Emerging ravenously hungry from their dens, if the land is still covered in snow, the bears — their shaggy coats ranging in colour from fawn to dark brown — scratch the ground into what looks like ploughed fields in their search for roots and tubers.

They are frequently thought of simply as meat-eaters, but bears, like humans, will consume almost anything. They are efficient scavengers. They relish some forms of garbage, and the putrified carcasses of domestic livestock.

During the year they'll feed on fungi, plants and grasses rich in protein and even certain insects — all part of the process of building themselves up for the next marathon snooze. And they'll get mildly drunk on alcoholic wild strawberries.

They will eat colonies of ants for their laxative effect. As the weeks go by, they may hunt small mammals and ground birds, or visit remote farmlands in search of food for themselves and their young. On such expeditions (principally under cover of darkness to avoid human enemies) they have been known to devour whole hives of honey, ignoring the bees inside and the stinging hordes

*Fifty years ago, bear hunts were frequent and "Bear Stew"
was a traditional dish in Asturias. Today, they top Spain's
endangered species list.*

around them.

Bears are expert tree-climbers, scrambling up the trunks to
shake sweet chestnuts and fat acorns out of the branches. In
summer, they feed heavily off bilberry bushes, running their paws,
with open claws, through the leaves and stuffing themselves with
the fruit.

And the bears fish among the white waters of mountain streams
that tumble over dark, gleaming rocks. Belly-flopping into the
torrent, they pin down a salmon with their paws before bringing
the writhing prize to the bank in their jaws.

UNTIL weaned, the cubs follow the sows everywhere, braving rough stream crossings and cuffs from older bears. The cubs' mortality rate can be as high as 40 per cent, having regard, among other things, to the mother's thin life in spring. By the second or third spring the blue-eyed youngsters are on their own, carrying out fishing expeditions without training. They have learned their lessons watching the others fish, but before they are ready to use their own skills they will scour the river-banks for the remains of salmon or trout left by the dominant, older bears.

Among recurrent myths about brown bears is that they have poor eyesight. It may not be as acute as their other senses, but they can, in fact, detect movement over long distances — an attribute essential to survival, as well as good fishing.

Another widespread belief holds they are notoriously unpredictable and, as such, dangerous. Contrarily, it has been established that the animals behave according to strict rules, based on size and consequent social rank. Each Spanish brown bear possesses a distinct personality, according to researchers; and although typecast, along with others, as savage and aggressive because of its size, it is by nature a retiring being.

All of the bear species can survive both extreme cold and blistering heat. As proved by their survival in Spain against lethal odds, the brown bear is adaptable and resilient, shaped by a hazardous evolution to be a wary opportunist.

While bears and man in general do not have a happy history of co-existence, the Spanish breed has some worthy allies — more than 14,000 of them. They are the members of a thriving wildlife conservation organization in Asturias, where the largest number of bears struggle to exist. Created by a dedicated Spaniard in his thirties, Roberto Hartasánchez of Llanes, it is known as *El Fondo en Asturias para la Protección de los Animales Salvajes* (FAPAS) and, with a brown bear as its emblem, has gained international

*Until they're weaned, bear-cubs follow their mother everywhere. It's a tough life, and the mortality rate can be as high as 40 per cent.*

recognition.

With their subscriptions and donations, members of all ages and both sexes throughout Spain and in several other countries finance FAPAS's bear protection campaigns and pay added compensation to farmers who *prove* to the provincial government they have suffered bear damage.

One of their volunteer wildlife wardens is Roberto's slim and wiry younger brother, Alfonso, whose guardianship of the bears is conducted over a wide region in a four-wheel-drive safari vehicle bearing the FAPAS crest.

Alfonso's base is a centuries-old hamlet of red-tiled roofs and clog-wearing villagers set among snow-capped mountains.

*A bear's paw print, next to a human boot print, gives an idea of the animal's size. Weighing up to 500 lb. the seven-foot Brown Bear is one of earth's largest land animals.*

There, until he died in late 1988, lived the bears' best friend, another animal: a handsome and highly intelligent Alsatian dog named Otto. He was, as far as I know, the world's first canine "bear-sniffer".

Having been specially trained for the job with Alfonso, Otto worked for years detecting whether or not a bear had been responsible for, say, killing a lamb, ravaging a maize-patch or tearing down a farm outhouse. Otto knew the bears' scent and recognized in an instant their spoor and scratch marks. Had no bear been around, Otto would give no whining nor tail-wagging signal.

In this way, the dog saved the government millions of pesetas every year. The authorities accepted that Otto revealed all spurious claims for payment. In turn, the bears were spared the vengeance of mistakenly outraged country folk.

Otto, as I discovered on an expedition with him and Alfonso, was worth his weight in gold.

His handler told me then: "Brown bears are peaceful. Unprovoked attacks are unknown."

It was essential, he added, they were left undisturbed or they might attempt to retreat further, and even give up breeding.

His brother, Roberto, adds: "Some people fear bears more than they need. And respect them not enough."

For an essay competition among thousands of Spanish children, the FAPAS head appealed: "Remember, the brown bear is a symbol of our independence, courage and pride." Despite such tactical pleas and the protective measures now provided, there are many who fear the bears of the Cordillera Cantábrica may no longer be around by the year 2000.

# CHAPTER TWELVE
# 'Wild West' Shows

O N my desk at home there's a 10-inch-long hank of ebony-black hair taken from a stallion's tail, a constant reminder of a hectic adventure in the Spanish countryside.

During high summer every year "cowboys" of all ages — from 16 to 60 — of the rugged Galicia region round up thousands of wild horses, the eager participants displaying their skill by wrestling the animals to the ground or riding them bare-back, rodeo style.

Several isolated villages are involved on different days in this unique and dramatic fiesta known as the *Rapa das Bestas;* principally Sabucedo, La Valga and Torrona.

Everywhere they are held in Galicia, these are thrilling but often perilous affairs with serious injury, even death, on the cards for the seemingly fearless "cowboys". Country people and foreign visitors alike lustily cheer on the men and youths who risk bites from enraged and frightened beasts, heavy blows from flailing hooves, or being trampled underfoot. Yet major casualties in these Spanish versions of "Wild West" shows are surprisingly few — whether the bare-chested participants are dragging down a horse by gripping its mane and fore-lip or spending a few seconds in a tempestuous ride astride a jack-knifing fury.

Extinct elsewhere, the hardy creatures of the mountains and rolling moorlands, of the heather and gorse, are corralled for a day annually in a spectacle believed to be hundreds of years old.

The adult *garranos,* as they are known, are driven miles from their pastures towards a hamlet of white-walled cottages. Their flowing tails and long manes are painlessly clipped with steel scissors, to provide ultra-fine hairs for artists' brushes. Meanwhile, the foals are driven apart from their mothers by the score of young boys wielding long sticks and flourishing bamboo canes. In separate pens, before being allowed to rejoin their parents at the end of the day, the young horses are lightly branded.

The main interest of the onlookers, however, centres on a stockade of stone walls that will become a dusty boiling pot of men, boys and animals.

Perched on a milestone on a misty dawn at Sabucedo, I followed through binoculars the horsemen expertly at work among the far-distant equine groups. With skills and timing born of many years of experience, the riders first enclosed each huddle

*Previous pages: a maelstrom of wild horses during Galicia's annual Rapas das Bestas, when villagers round up the horses that live in the surrounding country.*

of restive animals in a semi-circle, then with sharp cries and cantering feints nudged them towards the crowded village.

I had moved to a vantage point just outside Sabucedo as lines of driven horses converged to form a torrent streaming down towards me from the foothills, nostrils flaring and tails streaming. It was an awesome, terrifying sight.

And, transfixed, it seemed inevitable I would be crushed below the thundering hooves. But at the last moment the charge divided before me, and galloped past harmlessly on each side.

Later, I gazed down from a hillside churchyard on to a large natural bowl which became a maelstrom of raw power — made up of leathery, sweating "cowboys" and rearing, wildly whinnying *garranos*. The melée was punctuated by hoarse cries and the thudding sticks of the herders.

Meanwhile, youngsters threaded their way in and out of the crush of men and horses, calmly filling their plastic buckets with fistfuls of hair as the scissors went to work in the hands of those holding down the heaving, prostrate beasts.

An old Sabucedo villager at my side — pausing only now and then to shout encouragement to his middle-aged son grappling with a huddle of horses in the ring — told me *his* story associated with these folklore festivals.

It appears that in the dim past the good people of Sabucedo turned their work-horses loose into the uplands as a thanksgiving to the saints at the end of a terrible plague that claimed lives in every family. The animals seething and struggling in temporary captivity before us were, he claimed, descended from those set free as a holy sacrifice.

There are other equally touching legends attached to herds of *garranos* whose present-day counterparts are, in most instances, owned by individual land-holders or the Church. You can take your pick of these rich and romantic stories but, more prosaically, scientists claim the ecologically important breed of *Garrano*

*Roaming free in the Galician foothills, the Garranos are thought to be descendants of the original wild horses of Iberia.*

galaico is a "living testimony of *Equus ferus,*" said to have been the true wild horse of Iberia.

UP to 1973, little had been written about the *garranos* and their origins. In that year, however, a Spanish veterinarian named Iglesia Hernández produced a long professional thesis on them, stating there were exactly 21,690 of the animals in 35 different populations, scattered over Galicia, with marked genetic diversities.

The numbers are thought to be less today.

The Sabucedo round-up I attended — these affairs are listed as *curros* in Spanish calendars of events and booklets given to foreign tourists — was signalled in the early morning by rockets bursting overhead like anti-aircraft shells. Crows and sparrows burst from the trees.

And the rockets brought out every villager, all in festive mood. The girls wore gaudy dresses and silken ribbons with the national colours. Schoolboys postured, and adopted bullfighter stances in anticipation of the tumultuous circus to come. Greybeards swapped reminiscences of round-ups past. Mothers wheeled their babies to vantage points providing safe spots from which to watch the pageant. Ice-cream merchants and balloon sellers mingled with the crowds.

An hour later, youths and girls in traditional Galician costumes of crimson jackets, white ruffles on their leggings, appeared on the cobbled streets. Seemingly tireless, they marched up and down playing goat-skin bagpipes, pounding seasoned drums and singing songs in praise of the *rapa* and all those who would take part.

By the end of their performances the clamour and excitement of the round-up had begun. As the horses flooded into the corral a 13-year-old piper from the band stood on the rim, grimly trying to make his reedy notes heard above the din.

Lunch in the afternoon brought a short break to the hectic carnival. The blue-grey smoke of wood fires in the fields under oak trees drifted towards cotton-wool clouds in the still summer air. Steaks were grilled on hot stones, and I shared a pickled octopus tentacle with one of the men who had played a leading role in that morning's rodeo.

He chewed his portion with obvious relish, then turned to me.

"Why do we do it, *señor?*" he said rhetorically. "To you it must seem madness. But it's in our blood, since boyhood. Everyone proud of his manhood wants to join in. It's an honoured tradition. No one would dream of refusing to take part."

In the pen we approached a huge, now-docile stallion and my companion gently turned back a lip of the animal to display a set of white teeth more healthy than some domestic horses I had seen. The stallion's flanks were glossy with fitness.

It appears the wild horses react with spirit to any attempt to domesticate and saddle them. They have been known to sicken and die away from the hills.

Their hair, I was informed, had helped to produce masterpieces of art over the ages. This left me wondering if great men like Picasso, the most famous artist of the 20th century, used such delicate brushes in their studios — providing something of a link between the near-primitive and modern cultures.

# CHAPTER THIRTEEN

# Cameos

T HE Spanish skies are full of colour. And some of
Spain's birds are rare indeed.

The egg-stealing, AZURE-WINGED MAGPIE
inhabits only two places on earth, thousands of miles
apart: eastern Asia and the Iberian peninsula.

This species of the bird has wings and tail which reflect the
vault of heaven, and a black cap and white throat. It's sometimes
glimpsed flashing through an olive grove or a pine or eucalyptus
wood, calling to its mate with shrill "shrees." It may be pecking
at the fruit in an orchard, or less often visiting a garden.

Quieter and more secretive in the breeding season, the magpie
pairs build an open nest in the fork of a cork-oak or pine tree, and

*Kingfisher*

produce an average of three to four fledglings.

The KINGFISHER of the rivers and waterways is equally alluring, cloaked in irridescent blue and emerald green with a long, sharp bill and small, bright-red feet.

High, piping "cheeps" warn bird-lovers to approach slowly and silently the kingfisher perched on a riverside tree stump, scanning the tranquil waters.

With rapidly beating wings, the bird hovers for a moment or two above a ripple where a fingerling is feeding. A swift dive; the bill pierces the surface like a dagger, and a silvery, struggling fish is carried off to the nest in a deep burrow bored into a bank of the stream.

The splendour of the BEE-EATER's plumage rivals that of the other two birds. It is decked out in blue-green, a brilliant yellow, and black and brown feathers.

The bee-eater is often on display in many parts of Spain; almost as if aware of his handsome silhouette, the bird perches for long periods on telegraph wires and fences.

It flies with elegant, gliding turns on long, pointed wings, skilfully hunting and snatching insects in the air.

Bee-eaters like bush country with few trees, but they are also found in woodland glades.

Like the kingfisher, they breed in holes in river banks, or cuttings and sandpits.

Cross-sections of nesting sites have shown the mother has to struggle out backwards after feeding bees to the chicks.

Insects are of no interest to the OSPREY of southern Spain, but it shares a pervading interest in fish with the kingfisher.

Eagle-like and savage in contrast to gentle songbirds, the

*Bee-Eater*

*Cormorant*

osprey makes a dramatic kill.

I watched this once. I first spotted the bird flying slowly on brown wings 25 feet above a lake. Suddenly, it plunged, feet first, into the mirrored surface and seized a good-sized carp in its claws.

Wings beating rhythmically, the osprey made off towards the hills with its prize, calling triumphantly to its mate in high-pitched whistles. The male had every reason to hurry home. Bird viewers say the longer he spends away from the nest in search of food the greater the chance he'll be cuckolded. The eyrie-owner, it appears, is likely to be the last male to mate with the female just before egg-laying.

The best fisherman of rocky parts of the Spanish coast is a winter visitor, the bluish-black CORMORANT. On a river in

China, I saw cormorants, loosely tethered at the neck by a long cord, plunging into the coffee-brown current time and again to bring back in their beaks fish for their owners. At the end of the day, each bird was allowed to eat a fish or two as its reward.

Between dives, cormorants perch upright on rocks or poles, holding a spread-eagle pose with half-extended wings. Seemingly, this is a drying-out process.

The birds are sociable, usually flying fast in line or "V" formations, uttering low, guttural cries.

Equally keen-eyed but no fisher is the PEREGRINE FALCON. Slate-grey, with pointed wings, a blackish crown and distinctive buff-white spotted breast, it's one of the most formidable birds of prey in existence — popular with Arab falconers. As a result, its eggs are keenly sought by nest-robbers. But they now risk stiff prison terms. Under the first sentence of its kind in Spain, a Frenchman was sent to gaol for four months for stealing six peregrine (and two golden eagle) fledglings.

The peregrine hunts by hanging motionless in the southern Spanish skies, head to wind, before swooping on its prey almost vertically, at terrific speed. The slow, bewildered victims — pigeons, starlings, young grouse, goslings and other birds — have little chance of escaping that blurred, lethal dive of over a hundred miles an hour. There are those who believe the bird to be capable of a maximum stoop speed of 250 miles an hour. But quite how these predators manage to pull out of such a dive, avoid blacking out and actually see a target at such a lightning speed is unknown.

Between meals, the peregrine shows itself to be an accomplished glider.

Dignified in appearance, the female, larger than the male, is not too proud to use a disused crow's nest in a tree for her eggs and rapacious hatchlings. The nests are usually found in semi-open country with trees, or on cliffs.

*Kestrel*

Outside the breeding season, peregrines may range over marshes and moors with swift and strong flights with rapid wing-beats. Or they may be seen perching on poles or boulders near a river or lake.

The peregrine's numbers have been greatly reduced over the years. The effects of poisonous chemicals on its prey are thought to be the chief cause of blame for this mournful situation.

In happier times for the bird, peregrines were the favourites of Spanish kings and aristocrats in their pursuit of falconry.

It's a blood sport with gruesome kills and some modern falconers in the west, using dead, day-old chicks tossed high into the air, now limit exhibitions by the birds to displays of aerobatics.

World championships were held in the La Alcarria district of Guadalajara a quarter of a century ago when falconers from 17 countries showed the prowess of their birds.

On that day, Spain's 24-year-old chief falconer put his bird through a series of intricate manoeuvres before wagging a finger to bring it dive-bombing to a soft landing on his gloved fist.

"Falconry," he said in a victory interview, "is the union of two hunters — man, the most powerful being on earth, and the falcon, the most complete hunter in the sky."

Pointing to the bird, he added: "This beautiful creature is not my slave, but my friend — a willing partner in the hunt."

Another member of the falcon family is the KESTREL, the male of which species has a grey-blue head, spotted chest and chestnut upper parts.

Head to wind, it hovers for long periods high above open agricultural country before slanting down steeply to catch fieldmice and beetles.

It too may use an old nest, of a crow or magpie. On rare occasions it has become a town dweller — in the remains of a roof on a ruined building or a hole in a high wall where it will share life with those who dread the peregrine: the pigeons and the sparrows.

ELEONORA'S FALCON, inhabiting Robert Graves' "paradise" island of Mallorca, bears a royal title from the past.

The bird is named after one of the few famous women of the 14th century — Princess Eleonor, a distinguished Regent and war leader of Sardinia.

The name given to the alluring falcon living and breeding on Spain's island is to commemorate that of this remarkable and humane woman in history.

In 1392 she issued a law safeguarding the falcons around her. This measure, according to one chronicler, also "protected the honour, life and property of people." The bold and courageous decree was promulgated during an age of barbarism.

Time moves on to the end of 1988 when Mallorca, the largest of Spain's Balearic islands, was chosen by *BBC Wildlife* magazine as one of the 16 best places around the world — "The Pick of the

Planet" — for bird-watchers to visit.

Far from the hordes of holiday-makers and leisure trade eyesores, Eleonora's bird ("that most elegant of falcons," according to the well-known doyen of nature photographers, Bruce Coleman) lives among the rocky cliffs of the island's wooded northern mountains.

Eleonora's falcon has a spotted breast similar to the peregrine, and at 15 inches is about the same size.

In full view, it looks even more aristocratic than the other falcons.

Some of the birds have a novel way of hunting, delaying their late summer breeding to do so. On their exceptionally long wings, the Eleonoras, facing the wind and keeping stationary, will hover for long periods in a line over land or sea. In this way, they form a deadly barrier to the shrikes, hoopoes, nightingales and other small birds on the migration route from Northern Europe to Africa.

The seasonal "aerial wall" is a specialized way of obtaining rich food for themselves or their chicks. The falcons kill swiftly, biting and twisting the victim's neck.

At other times, grasshoppers, cicadas, beetles and such insects are not ignored as sources of family food. When there are few small birds around, the adults will go out at dusk to seize and devour bats.

The Eleonora's call is a harsh "keya," sometimes rapidly repeated. And often heard over the wetlands surrounded by delightful Mallorquín windmills on the island's north-eastern coast. Bruce Coleman thinks this marshy 'jewel' could be worthy of World Heritage Site status. It was there he watched 10 of these fascinating raptors, the island's most famous species, zooming and snapping up dragon-flies.

*Genet*

S AFE from predators, winged or otherwise, snug in their
nest in a hollow tree-trunk are the winsome, ring-tailed
GENET kittens of the wild cat breed. Generally two or
three in a litter, the spotted genets are lithe and agile
relatives of the civet and mongoose.

Shorter-legged and slimmer than cats in general, the genet has
a handsome coat, big eyes, a sharp muzzle and long ears. My guess
is it was brought to Spain from Africa many, many moons ago as
a seaman's pet.

It frequents the woodland and scrub of the south and north of
Spain. Nocturnal, the genet roams far and wide, preying on mice
found in the woods, and other rodents, smaller birds and reptiles.
Insects and berries are on the menu when the normal diet is hard

*Barn Owl*

to find.

The genet is a true feline, moving with ease even among thorny bushes; swiftly climbing trees.

A sort of aquatic ichneumon, the elusive OTTER runs on land with a bounding gait but, with all four feet webbed, hunts in the water — an Olympic swimmer of the aquatic animal world — in its pursuit of fish.

Visiting one of Spain's old castles at night can be a terrifying experience — thanks to the BARN OWL whose high-pitched call has given rise to countless tales of ghosts and hauntings.

Its stark white, heart-shaped face and dark, liquid eyes coming out of the blackness with a wild shriek can be, at least, unnerving.

*Great Spotted Woodpecker*

In daylight, though, with its bold stare and hissing, snoring and yapping notes, it's an attractively off-beat creature.

The barn owl's wavering night-flight starts at dusk, and the search for rats, mice and other small rodents in ruins, farmyards, marshes and fields goes on until sunrise.

It breeds principally in farm buildings (hence the name), or church towers...

The nesting choice of chisel-billed WOODPECKERS is generally the resonant trunk of a tree, whether, according to the species and their location, in a coniferous forest in the mountains and highlands or an old orchard. As is generally known, holes are drilled high up in the trunk. Even one in a broad branch may provide a home for the family.

Of Spain's varied company of woodpeckers the crimson-headed breed of black plumage — *pic noir* — is particularly impressive.

The largest of its kind in Europe, as big as a rook, the black woodpecker is seen (and heard) in central and northern Spain.

Like the others, it uses its short, stiff tail and powerful toes to climb trees where, with loud and rapid drumming heard clearly from afar in the rural silence, it chips away the bark and digs out an oval nest-hole. It may uncover insects in the trunk which it retrieves with a long, thin and sticky tongue.

This busy, yellow-eyed bird has a heavy, undulating flight during which it is apt to sing stridently.

The nest-hole bored out in spring with all the force of a power-tool establishes the bird's territory and intention to mate and breed. The subsequent clutch of eggs ranges from four to eight.

Three other types of woodpecker — the green, great spotted and lesser spotted — live in Spain.

All are brightly coloured, the greater and lesser with a red cap, white and dark feathers, and other recognizable features. The green woodpecker is distinguished by a wild "laughing" cry.

It's always a thrill for bird-watchers to sight a woodpecker at work.

But the field researcher's prize is the quaint, timid and rare PURPLE GALLINULE — in fact, a rich, dark purple-blue glossed with turquoise on the throat and breast. Its long legs, bill and eyes are bright red and, strangely like the barn owl, its voice is a weird, hooting shriek.

Highly secretive and seldom seen out in the open, it lives and breeds in swamps with dense reed vegetation such as Doñana.

On the few flying expeditions it makes (in search of frogs and other wetlands' food for chicks deeply hidden), it's distinguished by dangling legs with long, clawed toes that allow it to walk through marshy ground, and across floating vegetation without sinking.

*Imperial Heron*

The female stands guard over the nest in the reeds while her mate is away hunting.

It's difficult for the layman to see why the striking Spanish IMPERIAL HERON *(Ardea purpurea)* is known in other countries as the purple heron. Its colours are chiefly brown, black and grey, though perhaps the dark parts of its plumage have a purplish sheen in certain lights. But it's not to be confused with the truly-purple gallinule.

The Spanish name seems more appropriate: this particular bird looks like a king among herons. With a black crown and crest, large feet and a long, chestnut neck boldly black-striped.

This, too, is a creature of the swamps and marshes. It prefers denser vegetation than other herons; it breeds and nests in colonies in thick reed-beds or, now and then, in marshland bushes.

It is shy like the gallinule, but this modesty is not shared by another exciting and lovely bird, the extrovert HOOPOE which,

*Hoopoe*

with a handsome fan-crest, barred black-and-white wing patterns and graceful curved bill, is proud and eager to show itself off to anyone on a country stroll. It is best seen in profile, and seems to sense that.

This delightful bird — its call is a deep "hoo-poo-poo" — can run swiftly on the ground yet appears to enjoy presenting itself on bushes, rocks or among deserted buildings.

The pairs nest in tree cavities or, occasionally, in ruins.

The best feature of the NIGHTINGALE is not its appearance — its feathers are a featureless brown — but, of course, its golden song. This is poured out night and day from such deep cover as tangled hedges, bramble bushes or the damp undergrowth of lowland woods.

That famous liquid song, glorious, loud and musical, is unforgettable. Otherwise, the nightingale is a drab and furtive fellow.

It would be hard, however, to find a creature more lacking in

*Desman*

physical charm, and with no voice to compensate him, than the DESMAN of the peaks and remote streams of the Spanish side of the Pyrenees.

The desman's distinction is that it's one of the rarest animals on earth.

Little known and intriguing, the size of a mole (to which it is related), this sightless, nocturnal rodent has a long, flattened, red-tipped snout, large, webbed hind feet, clawed front feet and a rat-like tail.

There's nothing like it in the animal kingdom.

This aquatic mammal, five inches long and rarely photographed, "hunts" the larvae of May caddis- and stone-flies on river beds. With lightning swimming dashes, it probes for food with its highly sensitive and facile proboscis.

A litter of about four young desmans — or should it be "desmen"? — occurs each spring, in crevices under rocks or holes in river banks.

*Fat Dormouse*

Unknown to science before the 19th century, the desman looks like something out of a nightmare.

Water pollution has driven it from the coastal valleys higher and higher into the sierras. Unwholesome as it looks, the barely surviving desman can only live in the purest water.

Says writer David M. Schwartz who has lived in the Pyrenees: "It would be tragic if this fascinating little animal were forced out of existence by a world that has hardly begun to make its acquaintance."

A quaint neighbour of the desman, 6,000 feet up, is the FAT DORMOUSE, or scientifically, *Glis glis*. It earns the former name by gorging constantly on seeds and nuts before a winter hibernation.

It goes underground or takes to a hollow tree to sleep through the snows and ice. Its globular nest of grasses will probably be high in a tree — containing four or five young (not yet) fat dormice.

In company with the desman and fat dormouse, few may have heard of *Uria aalge ibericus.* That's the handsome sub-species of the blackish-and-white GUILLEMOT which, upright on webbed feet, looks at a distance like a young penguin.

Even fewer people may know this sea-bird in future: it's listed as the fastest vanishing member of the guillemot species in the Iberian peninsula.

Thirty years ago ornithologists calculated a total of 20,000 in breeding colonies on ledges of steep cliffs and offshore islands of Spain and Portugal, the majority inhabiting coastal Galicia and other shores of northern Spain.

There are now, according to Galician naturalist Juan Carlos Cabrero Figuero, possibly only 95 to a 100 pairs left alive — rare entries in field observers' notebooks as the birds dive skilfully and seek their food under the waves.

The mass tragedy of these birds, an army gone, is once more attributed to our species.

There were days when boatloads of villagers would skirt the cliffs and islands shooting into the dense breeding sites with rifles just for the thrill of downing large numbers of the birds.

Few of the killers found them palatable. They are tough and taste strongly of salt and fish.

During later years (when such "hunting" became illegal) supertankers and other ships spreading oil during their voyages added to the toll. Such a deadly form of marine pollution still goes on, and there's little hope for a guillemot whose dark wings are glued together by crude.

Like others of the hapless great auk breed, *Uria aalge ibericus* of the sea and precipitous nesting sites flies in small flocks in lines above the waves.

Into the sunset?

# CHAPTER FOURTEEN

# Envoi

MAN, warns the Worldwide Fund for Nature, is now in a position to eliminate a third of all wildlife on earth within the next 50 years. This sombre statement by the leading international conservation agency underlines the vital importance of Spain as a sanctuary.

This fact was sharply underlined in spring of 1989. King Juan Carlos signed a historic charter for the protection of nature. It consisted of 41 clauses and listed heavy new penalties for the killing or capture of endangered wild animals and birds.

Elsewhere, over the ages hundreds of species have joined the dodo, extinct at our hands. These range from the giant pied-bill grebe of Guatemala — artificially-introduced fish ate their food — to the blue butterfly of Palos Verdes in California (its last-ditch meadow was bulldozed to make a baseball pitch and stadium).

Many others around the globe are on the verge of disappearing. For ever. The same way. From Indonesia's Komodo dragon to the pink pigeon of Mauritius.

"Almost interminable is the list of fauna we have exterminated in our brief but inglorious reign as a species," laments wealthy British naturalist John Aspinall.

And Prince Philip heads those who deplore the fact that the amounts of money spent on aid for "often disastrously insensitive development projects" are a thousand times greater than funds available to the wildlife conservation charities.

Novelist and essayist Doris Lessing thinks human beings have not yet evolved an understanding of their individual selves as merely parts of a whole. Nor achieved a conscious knowledge of humanity as part of nature.

Only together with his fellow creatures — animals, birds, reptiles — does man "strike a small chord in the Cosmic Harmony," she writes.

In other words, wildlife is part of the cycle of existence, and all wild animals help to maintain the delicate balance of nature essential to our life on earth.

Ecologist Norman Myers regards the present decline of entire ecosystems on earth as "the greatest single setback to life's abundance and diversity since the first flickerings of life almost four billion years ago."

These words, and those of all concerned with the preservation of nature, are echoed by Greenpeace, the long-established environmental pressure group which, completely independent of political parties anywhere, conducts dramatic, non-violent conservation campaigns.

Greenpeace claims man has caused the extinction around the world of more than 500 species — of animals alone.

It is, perhaps, fitting some closing words on the subject should come from the teachings of the late Félix Rodríguez de la Fuente, killed in a helicopter crash in the Canadian Arctic, who did so much to make Spaniards aware of their fellow beings of the wild.

"When people are fully convinced of the importance of natural things to our environment," he declared, "we won't need hunting laws or fauna reserves. Each individual will be a protector of animals."

It's a fine thought. By that time, its pages having grown bigger and bolder with each passing year, Spain may have become a great living encyclopaedia of wildlife.

*Following pages: dusk over the majestic Sierra Morena, the rugged mountains that separate Andalusia from Castile.*

# Bibliography

**Birds of Britain and Europe,** by Roger Peterson,
   Guy Mountfort and P A D Hollom (Collins, London)
**The Case of the Midwife Toad,** by Arthur Koestler
   (Hutchinson, London)
**The Country Life Guide to Birds of Britain and Europe,**
   by Bertel Bruun (Country Life)
**A Field Guide to the Reptiles and Amphibians of Britain
   and Europe,**
   by E N Arnold and J A Burton (Collins, London)
**Grzimek's Animal Encyclopaedia**
**Mammals of Britain and Europe,** by Richard Orr
   (Peerage Books)
**Marcos,** by Gabriel Janer Manila (Souvenir Press, London)
**The National Trust Book of British Wild Animals,**
   by John A Burton (Cape, London)
**Our Magnificent Wildlife** (Oxford University Press)
**Pyramids of Life,** by John Reader and Harvey Croze
   (Collins, London)
**Spain** (Baedeker)
**Spain** (Fodor)
**Wild Animals of Britain & Europe,** by Nicholar Arnold,
   Gordon Corbet and Denys Ovenden (Collins, London)

The works of Spanish photographer-naturalist José Luis
Rodríguez, and the writings of Miguel Delibes on the
Spanish lynx.

Magazines: *BBC Wildlife* (Bristol); *FAPAS* (Llanes);
*International Wildlife* (Washington); *National Geographic*
(Washington); *Natura* (Madrid); *Quercus* (Madrid); *Panda*
(Madrid)

# English-Spanish Glossary

The following is a list of the animals featured in this book, as well as some of the other species found in Spain, along with their names in Spanish.

## AMPHIBIANS (Anfibios)

Frog: *rana*
Midwife Toad: *sapo partero*
Toad: sapo

## REPTILES (Reptiles)

Adder: *víbora*
Chameleon: *camaleón*
Gecko: *salamanquesa*
Hognosed Viper: *víbora hocicuda*
Lizard: *lagarto, lagartija*
Snake: *serpiente, culebra, víbora, (pop) bicha*
Tortoise: *tortuga*
Turtle: *galápago, tortuga*
Viper: *víbora*

## BIRDS (Aves)

Azure-winged Magpie: *Rabilargo*
Barn Owl: *lechuza*
Bearded Vulture: *quebrantahuesos*
Bee-Eater: *abejaruco*
Black Kite: *milano negro*
Black Stork: *cigüeña negra*
Black Woodpecker: *pito negro*
Buzzard (common): ratonero común

Capercaillie: *urogallo*
Cormorant: *cormorán*
Crane: *grulla*
Cuckoo: *cuco, cuclillo*
Eagle: *águila*
Eagle Owl: *buho real*
Egret: *garceta, garcilla*
Eleonora's Falcon: *halcón de Eleonor*
European Crane: *grulla*
Falcon: *halcón*
Fish Hawk: *águila pescador*
Flamingo: *flamenco*
Golden Eagle: *águila real*
Goshawk: *azor*
Great Bustard: *avutarda*
Great Spotted Woodpecker: *pico picapinos*
Greylag Goose: *ánsar común*
Grebe: *zampullín*
Green Woodpecker: *pito real*
Griffon Vulture: *buitre leonado*
Guillemot: *arao*
Harrier: *aguilucho*
Hawk: *azor, halcón*
Hen Harrier: *aguilucho pálido*
Heron: *garza*
Hoopoe: *abubilla*
Imperial Eagle: *águila imperial*
Kestrel: *cernícalo*
Kingfisher: *martín pescador*
Kite: *milano*
Lammergeyer: *quebrantahuesos*
Lesser Kestrel: *cernícalo primilla*
Lesser Spotted Woodpecker: *pico menor*
Little Owl: *mochuelo*
Long-Eared Owl: *buho chico*
Magpie: *urraca*
Montagu's Harrier: *aguilucho cenizo*
Night Heron: *martinete*
Nightingale: *ruiseñor*
Osprey: *águila pescador*
Owl: *buho*
Partridge: *perdiz*
Pheasant: *faisán*
Purple Gallinule: *calamon*
Purple Heron: *garza imperial*
Quail: *codorniz*
Red Kite: *milano real*
Scops Owl: *autillo*

Shag: *cormorán*
Sparrowhawk: *gavilán*
Spoonbill: *espátula*
Stork: *cigüeña*
Turtledove: *tórtola*
Vulture: *buitre*

## MAMMALS (Mamíferos)

Badger: *tejón*
Bat: *murciélago*
Bear: *oso*
Boar (wild): *jabalí*
Brown Bear: *oso pardo*
Chamois: *gamuza, rebeco (sp. Cantabrian Mountains),
    Sarrio (sp. Pyrenees)*
Deer: *ciervo, venado*
Desman: *desman de los Pirineos*
Dormouse: *lirón*
Fallow Deer: *gamo*
Fat Dormouse: *lirón gris*
Ferret: *hurón*
Fox: *zorro*
Genet: *gineta*
Hare: *liebre*
Hedgehog: *erizo*
Ibex (Spanish): *cabra montés (cabra hispánica)*
Ichneumon: *meloncillo*
Lynx (Spanish): *lince ibérico*
Marmot: *marmota*
Marten, Pine: *marta*
Mole: *topo*
Otter: *nutria*
Pine Marten: *marta*
Polecat: *turón*
Rabbit: *conejo*
Red Deer: *ciervo*
Roe Deer: *corzo*
Squirrel: *ardilla*
Stoat: *armiño*
Weasel: *comadreja*
Wild cat: *gato montés, gato pardo*
Wolf (Spanish): *lobo (ibérico)*

# Spanish-English Glossary

## ANFIBIOS (Amphibians)
Rana: *Frog*
Sapo: *Toad*
Sapo partero: *Midwife Toad*

## REPTILES (Reptiles)
Bicha: *popular name for Snake*
Camaleón: *Chameleon*
Culebra: *Snake, applied to Grass Snake and non-poisonous snakes of the Colubridae family*
Galápago: *Turtle*
Lagartija: *small Lizard*
Lagarto: *Lizard*
Salamanquesa: *Gecko*
Serpiente: *Snake, Serpent*
Tortuga: *Tortoise, Turtle*
Víbora: *Viper, Adder*
Víbora hocicuda: *Hognosed Viper*

## AVES (Birds)
Abejaruco: *Bee-Eater*
Abubilla: *Hoopoe*
Aguila imperial: *Imperial Eagle*
Aguila pescador: *Osprey, Fish Hawk*
Aguila real: *Golden Eagle*
Aguilucho: *Harrier*
Aguilucho cenizo: *Montagu's Harrier*
Aguilucho pálido: *Hen Harrier*
Ansar: *Greylag Goose*
Arao: *Guillemot*
Autillo: *Scops Owl*
Avutarda: *Great Bustard*
Azor: *Goshawk; also applied to Hawks in general*
Buho: *Owl*
Buho chico: *Long-Eared Owl*
Buho real: *Eagle Owl*
Buitre: *Vulture*
Buitre leonado: *Griffon Vulture*
Calamón: *Purple Gallinule*
Cernícalo: *Kestrel*
Cernícalo primilla: *Lesser Kestrel*
Cigüeña: *Stork*

Cigüeña negra: *Black Stork*
Codorniz: *Quail*
Cormorán: *Cormorant, Shag*
Cuclillo: *Cuckoo*
Cuco: *Cuckoo*
Espátula: *Spoonbill*
Faisán: *Pheasant*
Flamenco: *Flamingo*
Garceta: *Egret*
Garcilla: *Egret*
Garza: *Heron*
Garza imperial: *Purple Heron*
Gavilán: *Sparrowhawk*
Grulla: *Crane*
Halcón: *Falcon, Hawk*
Halcón de Eleonor: *Eleonora's Falcon*
Lechuza: *Barn Owl*
Martín pescador: *Kingfisher*
Martinete: *Night Heron*
Milano: *Kite*
Milano negro: *Black Kite*
Milano real: *Red Kite*
Mochuelo: *Little Owl*
Perdiz: *Partridge*
Pico picapinos: *Great Spotted Woodpecker*
Pico menor: *Lesser Spotted Woodpecker*
Pito negro: *Black Woodpecker*
Pito real: *Green Woodpecker*
Quebrantahuesos: *Lammergeyer, Bearded Vulture*
Rabilargo: *Azure-Winged Magpie*
Ratonero común: *Common Buzzard*
Ruiseñor: *Nightingale*
Tórtola: *Turtledove*
Urogallo: *Capercaillie*
Zampullín: *Grebe*

## MAMIFEROS (Mammals)

Ardilla: *Squirrel*
Armiño: *Stoat*
Cabra hispánica: *Spanish Ibex*
Cabra montés: *Ibex*
Ciervo: *Red Deer, also applied to Deer in general*
Comadreja: *Weasel*
Conejo: *Rabbit*
Corzo: *Roe Deer*
Desman de los Pirineos: *Desman*
Erizo: *Hedgehog*

Gamo: *Fallow Deer*
Gamuza: *Chamois*
Gato montés: *Wild cat*
Gato pardo: *Wild cat*
Gineta: *Genet*
Hurón: *Ferret*
Jabalí: *Wild Boar*
Liebre: *Hare*
Lince: *Lynx*
Lirón: *Dormouse*
Lirón gris: *Fat Dormouse*
Lobo: *Wolf*
Marmota: *Marmot*
Marta: *Pine Marten*
Meloncillo: *Ichneumon*
Murciélago: *Bat*
Nutria: *Otter*
Oso: *Bear*
Oso pardo: *Brown Bear*
Rebeco: *Chamois (sp. Cantabrian Mountains)*
Sarrio: *Chamois (sp. Pyrenees)*
Tejón: *Badger*
Topo: *Mole*
Turón: *Polecat*
Venado: *Deer, Venison*
Zorro: *Fox*

# Index

A page number in **bold type** indicates a major reference to a given subject. A page number in *italics* indicates a photograph.

179

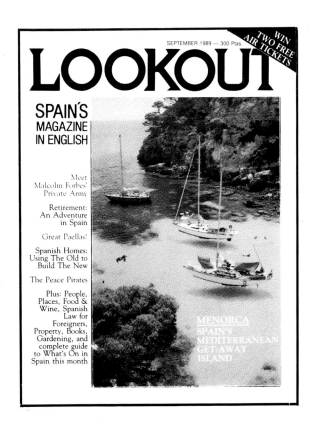

# Also from
# Lookout Publications

## Inside Andalusia,
## by David Baird. 200 pages (large format).

A travel adventure through Spain's most fascinating region, from the top travel writer in Spain today. David Baird invites you to explore an Andalusia you never dreamt of, to meet its people, and discover fascinating fiestas. Illustrated with brilliant colour photography.

## Here in Spain,
## by David Mitchell. 208 pages.

Spain seen through the eyes of famous travellers, from Borrow to Hemingway. This unique survey by David Mitchell, himself a respected observer of Spanish life, is a collection of the most outrageous, admiring, insulting, libellous, passionate, hilarious, thoughtful, bigoted, eloquent remarks ever made about any country. An invaluable key to understanding the Spanish character.

## Nord Riley's Spain,
## by Nord Riley. 270 pages.

The best of popular columnist Nord Riley's writing over 14 years, brought together in the funniest book ever published about expatriate life in Spain. If you're not one of those lucky expats living in Nord Riley's Spain, by the time you've finished this book you'll wish you were.

## Gardening in Spain,
## by Marcelle Pitt. 176 pages.

Your most valuable tool for successful gardening in Spain, from the author of Lookout Magazine's popular gardening column. How to plan your garden, what to plant, when and how to plant it, how to make the most of flowers, trees, shrubs, herbs. Illustrated with full-colour photographs.

## Cooking in Spain,
## by Janet Mendel. 400 pages.

The definitive guide to cooking in Spain, with more than 400 great Spanish recipes. Plus complete information on Spain's regional specialities and culinary history, how to buy the best at the market, a complete English-Spanish glossary with more than 500 culinary terms, handy conversion guide... all of it illustrated with colour photographs.

## 404 Spanish Wines,
## by Frank Snell. 140 pages.

From the author of the best-selling *202 Spanish Wines*, a guide to who's who on the wine shelf. What wines to buy, how to judge a wine, how to read the label, how to store your wine, how to serve it, and lots more.

## You and the Law in Spain,
## By David Searl. 216 pages.

Thousands of readers have relied on Lookout Magazine's best-selling You and the Law in Spain to guide them through the Spanish legal jungle. Now, author David Searl brings you a new, completely revised edition with even more information on taxes, work permits, cars, banking in Spain, buying property, Spain and the Common Market, and lots more. It's a book no foreigner in Spain can afford to be without.

*On sale at bookstores in Spain, or by post from Lookout Publications SA, Puebla Lucía, 29640 Fuengirola (Málaga), Spain.*